Walking in Rakeen's Shoes

Jennifer Rumler

For more information and further discussion, visit

Facebook.com/WelcomeTheStrangers

Cover art and design by

Rick Nease

www.RickNeaseArt.com

Published by Front Edge Publishing, LLC

For information about customized editions, bulk purchases or
permissions, contact Front Edge Publishing, LLC at
info@FrontEdgePublishing.com

In memory of Carol Rumler, the best mother-in-law
I ever could have been blessed with.

Contents

The Michigan State University Mission

In 1855, Michigan State University pioneered a bold "local experiment" that opened the doors of higher education and soon became a model for the nation that recognized the importance of higher education as a benefit to the public. Leadership at the university in the ensuing years has embraced, encouraged, and expanded the land grant mission globally with the question, "Who Will?" The answer? "Spartans Will."

As a public, research-intensive, land-grant university funded in part by the state of Michigan, our mission is to advance knowledge and transform lives by: providing outstanding undergraduate, graduate, and professional education to promising, qualified students in order to prepare them to contribute fully to society as globally engaged citizen leaders conducting research of the highest caliber that seeks to answer questions and create solutions in order to expand human understanding and make a positive difference, both locally and globally advancing outreach, engagement, and economic development activities that are innovative, research-driven, and lead to a better quality of life for individuals and communities, at home and around the world.

Acknowledgements

When a project like this comes to fruition there are many people whose love, friendship, collegiality, and support make it possible. To my three sons, the lights of my life: E.J., Chip, and John—thank you for your patience and encouragement—the journey would not be the same without you. Thank you to my four exchange sons, Thomas, Francesco, Nicolò, and Umberto, for opening the world up to our family. Thanks also to ACCENT International and the staff at the Rome Study Center, the Sales Leadership Minor, the Communication Department, the MSU Office of Study Abroad, the MSU Office of Service Learning and Civic Engagement, the Joel Nafuma Refugee Center, St. Vincent Catholic Charities' Refugee Resettlement, Lynn Aguado, Karin Hanson, Jill Drzewiecki, Daniela Morales, Piero Rijtano, Adama, Maiga, Lamin, Fahad, Nasim, Mohammed, Ron Leuty, Stephanie Henry, Karoline Kinjorski, Dmitri Barvinok, Judi Harris, John Karasinski, Abbie Newton, Brad Gakenheimer, Joe Grimm, the 2016 Romies, and Seàn-Patrick Lovett for so many things it would take a lifetime to enumerate! And finally, thank you to Rakeen for allowing us to share your life and your story.

The group outside the grotto in Vatican Gardens.

Introduction

He was quiet and shy when I first met him. He wore a T-shirt, jeans, tennis shoes, and strangely, a scarf, in May. He looked tired and a bit weary, but the kind smile never left his face. He was an artisan, and I was leading a study abroad program in Rome, Italy, accompanying twenty-five undergraduates from Michigan State University. His name was Rakeen.

We arrived shortly after noon. Several of the students were tasked with cooking an African dish. They were handed a recipe, and it would serve about twenty people for lunch. They were scared and nervous. *What if they ruined it? What if it didn't taste right?* Many of them did not even cook for themselves in their residence halls or apartments in East Lansing, let alone cook for such a large group (unless you consider frozen pizza, Ramen noodles, or boxed macaroni and cheese cooking). This would be their lunch, and they were cooking for the men who made up the group Artisans Together. Rome is a gorgeous, splendorous, complex city, but the artisans were not there on vacation, to see the sights, to take in the culture, or to experience several millennia of world history. The Artisans Together, the name evoking a scene from a bohemian artist's colony, instead, were homeless, jobless, political refugees.

Thus began my journey at the Joel Nafuma Refugee Center. That was three years ago. But how did we get from Point A to Point B? It all started when I asked the executive board of one of the student groups I advise, Global Sales Leadership Society, "What makes you global?" They responded that they wanted to get jobs with global companies. Not a bad goal, but what, indeed, made their group global? Really nothing. But if it was in the name, shouldn't we aspire to do something global? I then contacted the Dean's Designee for study abroad in our College (Communication Arts and Sciences), to see how we could create an international program, and "Made in Italy" was born.

When it first came to fruition, the program was four weeks long during the month of July. Well, if you have ever been to Rome in July, you would know the folly of our thinking. Every day the temperatures were between 90 and 100 degrees Fahrenheit. Italians are not famous for their use of air conditioning, and sleeping for Michiganders, as we're called, often required stripping down and applying wet washcloths to bare skin to stay cool. The classrooms were hot and the students' energy waned. Espresso was a good antidote for the listlessness, but it only seemed to increase our body temperatures. It was clear that I was a "newbie" to this thing called study abroad, and I had a lot to learn.

Admittedly, I had not been overseas, or even on an airplane, since my own study abroad experience as a graduate student at Michigan State University. I was awarded a scholarship from *Die Deutsche Akademische Austausch Dienst* (The German Academic Exchange Service) to study at the University of Regensburg in the southern German state of Bavaria. In 1990. Fast forward twenty years and here I was taking university students to a country I had never been to, one where I knew exactly three words in the national language: *ciao, pizza,* and *spaghetti.* It sounded crazy to me too, but I was always lecturing my students about expanding their comfort zones, doing things out of the ordinary, challenging themselves, and testing their mettle. I told them that putting themselves out there would help them excel, and it would set them apart from other students. How could I not follow my own advice and still maintain any credibility?

The program was a success but I couldn't help feeling a little empty when it was over. Here I was teaching students how to be effective salespeople, teaching them how to fetch an average starting salary of $56,000 a year (plus commission) and six figures within five years of graduation. But to what end? My students' financial success was a great accomplishment, but I still felt empty. What kept nagging at me was how many homeless people I saw in Rome: disabled people whose legs were mangled and twisted, who got themselves around by pushing themselves on makeshift skateboards; amputees who had nothing to make them ambulatory other than their calloused knuckles; a woman who laid prostrate on the *Ponte Sant'Angelo* (Sant'Angelo Bridge) for hours in the heat of the day with a small paper cup in front of her for spare change; the emaciated, rumpled, homeless street artist drawing masterpieces on the sidewalk, kept company only by his three starving dogs. No one ever mentioned them. No one seemed to notice them. No one seemed to care. And it bothered me. It bothered me a lot.

My students would meander through the city like rabid tourists, consuming all it had to offer. Taking photographs, mostly selfies, with monuments, landmarks, and statues, for which they had no inkling of the significance or history. Consuming the fashion districts, consuming the out-of-this-world Italian cuisine, consuming, consuming, consuming, like disinterested, disengaged tourists checking things off a predetermined bucket list. After a great amount of reflection and contemplation, I realized that I was the only one who could change how we interacted with the city that would be our home for six weeks. I would have to set the tone. I would have to put assignments and tasks before them to engender residency in Rome rather than haphazard tourism. I would have to engineer their experience. So I did.

The first year we worked at a soup kitchen sponsored by *Caritas* (charity) through the Diocese of Rome. The second year, we worked with *Ronda della Solidarietà* (Patrol of Solidarity), an organization that prepares food and takes it directly into the *piazze* (squares) to homeless people. Both experiences completely changed how the students interacted with the city, and how we interacted with one another. The first year the students were self-involved, self-absorbed, and self-centered; after introducing the service learning, they became human and humble and caring. They were appreciative and awakened to the vast world around them, a world larger and far more complicated than the East Lansing bubble they were living in.

Perhaps for the first time, they realized how fortunate and privileged they were. Previously, they never stopped to think that many of the world's citizens don't leave the ivy-covered halls of academia and begin earning such a generous salary. They never stopped to think that most people in the world do not have access to jobs, clean water, and stable food sources, let alone a college education. They never stopped to think that, for some, the biggest problem on a Friday night isn't deciding what outfit to wear or which designer shoes would best match. They realized how much they take for granted. They told me that if I hadn't assigned them the service learning, "that they never would have noticed the homeless people at all." They had a new purpose, and it wasn't self-gratification. They worked for the benefit of others, and they liked it. We had in-depth discussions about race, ethnicity, bias, prejudice, privilege, social justice, history, politics, poverty, government, human rights and the impact those things have on business. It became the most important, fulfilling work I have ever done. I felt like I became part of the human race, not just someone perpetuating the rat race. As many times as my students claimed that the program and working with the refugees had been life changing for them, the change that occurred in me was even more profound.

But, as often happens, there were still some obstacles. The volunteer coordinators and those we served at the soup kitchen and in the *piazze* spoke only Italian. While my students take a survival Italian class, they are nowhere near being fluent, and it became a huge source of frustration. They truly wanted to communicate with the people they were serving. Similarly, those being served were equally frustrated because they did not know much English. I then heard about a refugee center in the city where all of the volunteer coordinators and many of the guests speak English. That was three years ago. That was when I met Rakeen.

Jennifer Rumler is the Managing Director of the Sales Leadership Minor, a combined effort between two nationally-ranked colleges at Michigan State University, the Broad College of Business and the College of Communication Arts and Sciences. She has owned two sales-intensive businesses and has worked in student affairs, academic advising, recruiting, admissions, instruction, and instructional design. She was a fellow of the Adams Academy for Educational Excellence and Innovation, and is the founder and President of Welcome the Strangers, a non-profit organization for the benefit of political refugees. She has three sons and has hosted four high school exchange students, one from Germany and three from Italy. In her spare time she enjoys reading, gardening, listening to music, and spending time at Lake Michigan. LinkedIn: https://www.linkedin.com/in/jennifer-rumler-291b3b9.

Preface

They are referred to as refugees, immigrants and asylum seekers. Their lives are reduced to numbers, plotted on charts in global reports about migration.

We forget that they are human beings. Back in their home countries, many were respected community leaders and some were professionals: doctors, lawyers, professors, artisans and artists. Hidden behind the statistics on global migration are sons, brothers, fathers, daughters, sisters, mothers, husbands and wives. Each one has a unique story, a particular set of talents and a dream for the future.

In these pages, you will meet these often-faceless people. You will discover the personal side of this global news story that usually is underreported in mainstream media. You will meet Rakeen, the young Afghan refugee I met in Rome last summer when Jennifer Rumler first introduced me at the Episcopal Church of St. Paul's Within the Walls. Before that hot sunny afternoon, it had never occurred to me that the side gate of the church would lead to a place where different languages, traditions and religions were forming a diverse, supportive community. This is the Joel Nafuma Refugee Center, providing hospitality and assistance for refugees and asylum seekers from Afghanistan, Syria, Pakistan, Mali and many other Asian and African countries.

Rakeen's story is unique. It's also universal, because his experiences as a migrant mirror those of countless men and women—people we might glimpse in a TV news report about a dramatic rescue at sea. Across Europe and especially in Italy where I am based, we often notice migrants in the street, outside the train station or refugee center, on the bus, or at the supermarket. But, most of us never talk with migrants so we know next to nothing about their lives.

Our assumptions are based on what we may quickly observe and on the news reports we see or read. In 2017, those news reports are increasingly colored by the hot-button political disputes concerning immigration that are simmering in the United States as well as many parts of Europe. These political debates are reaching threatening tones in many parts of the world; they wind up spreading anxiety and stereotypes about these families.

The truth is that thousands of people are in need of international protection, each year. Many are trying to flee their home countries due to persecution, war and other forms of misery. This book focuses on immigration to Europe where migrants are either crossing the Mediterranean Sea on overcrowded boats or are traveling overland across the Western Balkan Peninsula. Whichever path they follow, they are undertaking long, dangerous journeys, often relying on smugglers and sometimes ending in death for loved ones as some of these families encounter unexpected catastrophes. As they travel, these families cross international boundaries, different cultures and languages—making their journey a pilgrimage that also challenges their sense of identity, culture and faith. This perilous journey is not over once migrants make it to Europe.

For countless families, Europe represents a chance for a brighter future—a hope so powerful that it prompts migrants to risk their lives in the journey. When they arrive, however, they discover a wide range of responses. First, there is the complex asylum process, which can take up to several years.

Meanwhile, migrants must struggle with new languages and cultural barriers as they try to rebuild their lives. On a daily basis, they are confronting a wide range of responses to their arrival in Europe from the anger of xenophobia, Islamophobia and racism—to the warm-hearted acceptance of many Europeans who believe in humanitarian assistance, dialogue and global solidarity.

Through news reports, we hear more about the tragedies and the angry responses than we do about the acceptance. What makes this new book so valuable is the welcoming doorway it represents into the incredible network of helpful associations, charities and individual citizens working to assist refugees and migrants. In a time when many world leaders seem intent on throwing up new barriers, such positive stories of peaceful coexistence are inspiring and absolutely essential if we are to see real men, women and children behind the slogans and statistics.

Rakeen's story will help readers understand what it means to face food insecurity, forced displacement, and all of the enormous psychological and emotional consequences of forced migration. Through political debates about immigration in news media and social media, this year, millions of people around the world are only encountering images of migrants and refugees as one end of an "Us vs. Them" tug of war. *Walking in Rakeen's Shoes* helps readers discover they have a lot more in common with immigrants than we might have imagined. The book is a powerful testament to friendship, respect and sharing.

Through this book, the Michigan State University students who travelled with Jennifer Rumler to Italy are inviting us to uncover the commonalities and the compelling human stories as the students discovered them in their own encounters with migrants and refugees. Along the way, *Walking in Rakeen's Shoes* also is an opportunity to see Rome through Rakeen's eyes. In this perspective, the streets, monuments and geography of Italian and European cities and villages acquire new meanings and functions, especially in the maps created by refugees according to their needs and experiences.

Beyond our personal responses to this book—and you will feel that emotional connection as you move through these pages—*Walking in Rakeen's Shoes* is a valuable tool for education about what is emerging as one of the most important issues in global politics and planning today. I encourage you to read the book, then share it with friends. Consider discussing this book with your small group, perhaps a class or book club you attend.

Ultimately, this is a story of hope and determination, glimpsed through Rakeen's experiences and through the voices of the students who share their honest responses with us. In these pages, many different lives are coming together to raise a collective voice for the voiceless.

As that collective voice rises, we realize that we share many of the deepest questions that motivate these men and women who risk everything to journey toward a new life. We discover that all of us are asking: What is home? What is equality? What are human rights?

Together, we are asking: How can we build a more peaceful world together? How can we continue to live and work with our own families, friends and colleagues—yet also reach out to the many men, women and children who find themselves in need?

Elisa Di Benedetto is a journalist based in Italy with a special focus in her reporting on religion, migration and cultural diversity. She has earned degrees in communication studies, peacekeeping and security studies—and has reported from Afghanistan, Lebanon and Kosovo. Her work has been honored by groups including the Overseas Religion Reporting Fellowship of the International Center for Journalism and the Henry Luce Foundation Promoting Excellence in Global Coverage of Religion Program. Elisa Di Benedetto is a founding member of the International Association of Religion Journalists where she is Co-Managing Director and web editor at www.TheIARJ.org.

Mackenzie Van Vleck and Shelby Roland
in the throes of a giggle fit.

Strangers in a Strange Land

THE STUDENTS ARRIVED in Rome jetlagged, tired, yet extremely excited to spend their first morning getting acclimated. Following a short walking tour of the immediate neighborhood surrounding the ACCENT Rome Study Center, twenty-two of us crammed onto the #40 bus from Piazza Chiesa Nuova to St. Paul's Episcopal Church for our volunteer orientation. I had been looking forward to this moment for many months. It would be my first opportunity to see my three Muslim "sons" in a year, Adama and Maiga from Mali, and Rakeen from Afghanistan, whose story will unfold in the following pages. This being my fourth year working at JNRC, I was anxious to see "my boys," especially since I knew that Adama postponed his leaving for Paris to try to find work, putting his newly-acquired driver's license and his native French tongue to use, until after we had seen each other. Hugs, kisses, long embraces ensued as the students witnessed our mutual affection for each other. Last year the three started calling me their "Mom," which I consider a huge honor, knowing how much their own mothers meant to them. I gave them all MSU Spartan T-shirts and they didn't waste a second putting them on so we could all take pictures together. But of course, we told them they couldn't wear the shirts if they didn't know the significance. The colors for Michigan State Spartans are green and white, and often one of the cheers during football or basketball games involves one side of the stadium or arena shouting, "Go Green!" while the other side shouts in response, "Go White!" It has been my experience that no matter where you are in the world, Spartans will always recognize other Spartans—train stations, restaurants, hotels, and on the street—and my boys needed to know how to react when confronted with someone shouting, "Go Green," at them while wearing their shirts. Then the students and I sang the Spartan fight song and afterward I was immediately instructed by Adama, Maiga, and Rakeen to send them the words because they wanted to understand what it was all about.

After our hellos we went to the second floor of the church for our orientation. I met a new-comer to the Center, Lamin, from The Gambia. He is smart, funny, articulate, and was applying to John Cabot University, an American University in Rome, with the help of the American Embassy. He did not disclose many details about his journey from Gambia to Rome, but we all knew by watching the emotions play across his beautiful dark face that it was a harrowing journey, one that involved his being detained and sent back several times by human traffickers demanding money, only to escape again.

In order to best orient the students to the people they were going to meet and work with, the volunteer coordinator, Rakeen, Maiga, and Lamin all told parts of their stories, and for the first time, this nebulous global refugee situation that the students had been hearing about over the past several months in our pre-departure meetings became real. They were able to see the faces, to learn the names, to hear the stories from those individuals who had lived through it, and who survived to tell their tales. They told us so we would tell others and spread the truth about this situation from one person to another until people understand that these men are not terrorists. They are not members of ISIS. They are not part of Al Qaeda. They are not part of the Taliban. They have no interest in taking jobs away from anyone. They do not desire to become a burden on any country's economy. They simply want to live in peace and safety, to provide for themselves, to get an education, and to earn a living. They left corrupt war-torn countries to avoid the same extreme factions that fill us with terror. Only for us, it is an unexperienced terror, one that we learn about vicariously through television screens and news media, exacerbated by political rhetoric suggesting we build walls and ban Muslims. All of the guests at JNRC have looked death in the face. They have indeed been terrorized. Some of them bear physical scars, but all of them bear unseen, persistent, emotional scars.

After the students were able to get a bit of rest, settle into their apartments, and get the lay of the land, we returned to JNRC at 8:00 am the following Friday to participate in "A Day in the Life of a Refugee" tour I had arranged for the students, but also for my own edification. Five refugees ranging in age from 23 to 32 took us on a tour of the city. This was not a tourist tour. They took us to the places a refugee would typically have to go in order to become registered with the police, and for services such as meals, clothing, and other basic necessities. They also took us to places where they would go to find a quiet place to sit, a place to sleep, and some sense of security. My group went with Rakeen and, according to my pedometer, we walked fifteen miles in our attempt to simulate what a refugee goes through on a daily basis, what they refer to as being *sempre in giro* (always turning). We returned to JNRC five hours later hot, tired, thirsty, overwhelmed, emotionally drained, and with very sore feet. The students could not have asked for a more realistic "Day in the Life" tour:

I'm almost ashamed of how little I knew before I came here. I thought refugees were mostly homeless people living in urban, deserted, undeveloped areas with little understanding of technology. But many leave to flee the government. Many are educated in many languages; Maiga knows 6. We are all alike in that we seek love, compassion, education, and a safe place to call home.

—Anna Mazzara

The "Day in the Life of a Refugee" tour really put the work that I will be doing on this program into perspective. Our guide, Maiga, is one of the most sensitive and positive people I have ever had the pleasure of being around. He started off by taking us to the Termini station, and explained to us the true struggles of refugees in Italy. Not only are they struggling with their basic human needs but they are also forced to find their own way to get the necessary papers to stay in Italy. Every day Maiga and refugees like him have to find ways to eat and drink and wash their clothes without any support system or comprehension of the language that surrounds them. We came to a small park near the Coliseum and Maiga had us all sit down and listen. It was very quiet and peaceful, which is the reason he would go there during the day to just relax and think. He told us about the importance of a positive mindset. As you can imagine, most refugees do not have a positive outlook. After all the struggle and pain they endure in their lives it almost always leaves them bitter and sad. Maiga told us that he was that way until he came to Italy and found the church. It was there his eyes were opened to a world of caring people and open hearts and he adopted a positive persona because he knew that is what this world needs. I am excited to do whatever I can to help. If every refugee is half as kind as Maiga, then they deserve all the help that we can give.

—Zane Wilson

Before we got to JNRC, I did not know what to expect at all. My group was matched up with a 24-year-old man from Afghanistan, named Mansur. He has been living in Italy for just over a year. We began walking from JNRC and our first stop was Centro Astalli, a refugee center where breakfast is served from 8:00-9:00 a.m., where refugees can use shower facilities, and request medicine. From there, we went back to different parks throughout the city where Mansur used to spend most of his days, sleeping, and meeting friends who were also refugees. There, he described that some of the parks would catch a trace of free Wi-Fi from the surrounding restaurants. Although he didn't have access to a device every day that he could utilize to browse the web, he was searching for jobs. Mansur informed me that recently the laws had gotten stricter in Rome for refugees. Just to have the slim chance of getting placed in government housing could take up to two to three months from the time of application. Mansur didn't speak Italian before coming to Italy, so he taught himself. Not knowing Italian was an even bigger barrier to finding a job, on top of the already tremendously steep 40% unemployment rate in Italy for 18-30 year olds. Mansur pointed out different spots where he would sleep in a patch of grass, under an awning, on a bench, or at different parks. I can't really compare what we have experienced on our program to what refugees have experienced. Our experience is an education; a refugee's is survival. I didn't ask Mansur how he got to Rome, partially because I was afraid of hearing the truth. Also, I didn't want to trigger unwanted emotions, fear, or memories of tragic experiences that he probably had. As our walk concluded, I felt closer to Mansur. He's a human being, just like me. He's hungry to learn, to experience more, and to try to better his situation. I really hate that there are so many assumptions made by people of all ages and all backgrounds that refugees are aliens to our society. Mansur is an extremely kind, genuine, young man that has enormous potential to make his life better. It was unbelievably difficult and uncomfortable to even get a glimpse into his "day in the life."

—Tyler Kramer

Rome is the farthest I have ever been from my home and family. When I was accepted to attend this study abroad experience I had no idea how it would change my life. We complain so much back home. We complain about the food we have, our homes, cars, and whatever else we can think to complain about. Being here and spending a day in the life of a refugee has been the most eye opening experience that I could ask for. I am nothing but grateful for everything that I have and the opportunities that I have had.

Growing up as a brown girl from a less privileged area of Detroit, I've always been considered to have less. This day has taught me that I do have so much more to be thankful for and to never take anything I have for granted. I spent the day with Ramin, who never stops smiling! He wanted to learn so much about our lives and us. He taught us some Italian and about being a trendy dresser, he gave us fashion advice. The first place Ramin showed us was a shelter he needed to go to once he arrived. It's scary because there are no billboards saying, "get your documents here!" You just have to find that information out yourself. At the shelter, people can take showers and get a meal. He said thousands of people line up there daily for food. I could not imagine having to wait in line for hours to get the food I need for the day. At one point he gave us a choice between walking two hours and taking the metro. First reaction, we all said, "METRO!" After thinking about it and hearing him speak about how many hours he walks a day, we all felt horrible complaining even a little, but he is so full of joy and willing to help and give to others. For example, one person in the group forgot her bus pass and without hesitation he gave her one of his. These passes are not free and none of us expected him to do that. Though they are not expensive, as much as he travels they are necessary for him and he sacrificed it for her. Ramin feels privileged to be free and able to walk and get fresh air. We take even that for granted each and every day. He took us to this huge open field and we expected to see something amazing like you do at every corner in Rome. This field was completely empty. He said there was once a huge tent where he slept for a while but it was suddenly taken down after the Paris terrorist attacks for safety reasons. Though he never felt comfortable there or got a good night's rest, it was somewhere he could go and it was just taken away without warning. I then imagined living a life where I have no control. Ramin chooses not to speak too much about his experiences in Afghanistan. It seems hard for him. He plays guitar and is currently taking cosmetology classes. He has so much hope and is determined to work for a better life for himself. On our journey he pointed out his home to us. It was an apartment building with the Italian flag hanging from the roof. We asked about his living situation and he said he shares a room with three other men, has a shower, a bed, appliances, and can stay for up to six months. He then said, "I have everything here." At this point I was holding back all of my tears. For him to be so grateful for this and for Americans to be so constantly selfish was so unbelievable to me. I've always had those things and I've never once truly felt like I had everything! I am truly inspired by stories like Ramin's and I am so happy to be able to work at the center and give back.

—*Tery Bradshaw*

Rakeen took us around and showed us places where he used to sleep, most of which were parks, and I began to understand at a very basic level how extraordinarily difficult the life of a refugee is. He told us about how he and other refugees would have to hide from the police because if they were caught in the parks, they would be kicked out. But of all the things and places that Rakeen showed us, the most powerful part of the whole experience was when he took us to a park overlooking the Coliseum. After walking through tall grass, we came to a spot with a tree near the edge of the park area with a beautiful view of the Coliseum. It was here that Rakeen told us how he came to be in Rome. I've never heard a sadder story in my entire life, especially not directly from the very person who has experienced all this pain. Then he said something to me that will stick with me forever. He looked out over the masses of people milling around the Coliseum and said, "One day I hope to be those people. I hope that I can bring my family to these places and be a tourist just like them." That hit me hard. Something that I was taking for granted— the fact that I could go and see these beautiful monuments and then return home with stories to tell— is something that Rakeen hopes for every day. Rakeen is not a bad person. In fact, he's one of the nicest, most genuine people I've ever met. He doesn't deserve what's been done to him, but he doesn't let that stop him from hoping and having faith. When I think about my perceptions of refugees previous to meeting Rakeen, I am disgusted with myself. I just assumed they were dirty, sad, hopeless people who had been dealt a terrible hand in life. And although I was right about their unjust fate, I was completely wrong about the people themselves. These people are no different than anyone else. They laugh and smile and know how to have fun. They dress normally and wish to live a normal happy life. Yes, they've experienced tragedy beyond most Americans' comprehension, but they are still hopeful. Rakeen showed me how similar I am to him or any other refugee. He showed me that the bad things that happened to him don't define him. The daily struggles that he and all refugees endure are heartbreaking. After just spending a half-day with him, my feet hurt from walking so much, but despite the things he has to do every day simply to survive, he still finds energy to smile and laugh and hug people he's just met. Rakeen and I are both strangers in Italy. We are in two completely different situations, but nonetheless we are both strangers. We both love the game of chess. I miss my family because I haven't seen them in months; Rakeen misses his family. We are similar in so many ways but completely different in others. The thing is that because of our similarities, Rakeen and I can connect. That's something that I think most people who have no experience with refugees don't understand. Through our friendship we each have something of value to give to each other. Rakeen has taken me around Rome and shown me things that I would never have found on my own. I am truly a stranger in a strange land. I can't speak the language and I don't naturally fit into the lifestyle of most Italians, so I have to make an effort, just like Rakeen has had to do the last three years. From Rakeen I learned how fortunate I am to be able to have a place to call my home and to have a family who loves and cares about me, something many refugees no longer have. So no, Rakeen and I are not in similar life situations, but that doesn't mean we aren't similar. We are.

—*Matthew Wigglesworth*

The park opposite the Coliseum, where Rakeen
slept when he first came to Rome.

Bittersweet Dreams

RAKEEN DREAMS ABOUT his family. Recurring, wonderful dreams that comfort him and haunt him in turns. In his dream he smells the familiar smells of home, the sight of his mother in the kitchen, his four siblings chattering as they do their homework while he supervises. They look up to him. He is their big brother and he is a dutiful son who assists his mother with them, for his father is often out of town working as an engineer. There is nothing extraordinary about the scene. It is commonplace, routine, and comfortable. The sights, sounds, smells, and feelings of home life envelop him. Then he wakes and remembers that his family has been murdered.

The dream is often the same. His mother is cooking *mantu* (beef dumplings) or *ashak* (eggplant with yogurt sauce), two of his favorite dishes. He is helping his two little brothers, ages 12 and 11, and his two little sisters, 9 and 7, with their homework. He is haunted and anguished by the memories, because when he awakens, he realizes he is in his one-room apartment two and a half hours outside of Rome, a world away from his idyllic life in Kabul, Afghanistan.

He hasn't done his laundry for a couple of weeks because he's been working as a painter for the Beehive Ho(s)tel, owned by American couple Linda Martinez and Steve Brenner, to earn some extra money. When he works in the city he is able to stay the night so he doesn't have to go back and forth to his apartment risking missing the last bus out of town, and having to endure the long commute. Then he can begin painting again the next day.

His apartment has no stove or washing machine, so he eats his meals in the city or cooks on a hot plate. He washes his laundry by hand in the sink. He is tired, his arms and back ache, his hands are chapped, and the intensity of the loss of his family never seems to disappear. He tells everyone that he is fine, and he smiles through the pain, while inside, he despairs about how long he will have to be a refugee. So far, it's been seven years.

> According to the UNHRC, the average length of time a person spends in a refugee camp is 18 years.

The living space of a refugee in the park.

Rakeen takes the group to a field of grasses and wildflowers, where refugees regularly sleep on cardboard boxes. In the background stands the Coliseum.

The Tour

PRE-DEPARTURE MEETINGS FOR our program
begin in January, five months before we leave. This program
requires commitment, as does the Sales Leadership Minor,
which graduates experienced, ethical, effective, professional
salespeople. Neither program is for the faint of heart, because
doing the kind of business that sales requires, students have
to be willing to step out of their comfort zones every single
day. The first session is often a Q&A to answer the multitude
of questions parents have about their children leaving the
country on their own for the first time and an ice-breaker to
allow the students to begin to feel comfortable with those
they often become best friends with over the next several
months. We have a session with local representatives from
St. Vincent Catholic Charities in Lansing, one of a small
number of organizations in the United States that assists with
the relocation of refugees to provide a comparative frame of
reference. One session is a discussion based on books they
read over the semester break, one on refugee trauma and the

effects it has on its victims, the other a journal-style narrative about the Lost Boys of Sudan. I want the students not only to empathize with the guests at the center, but to feel what these people experience to the extent they can. One of my first thoughts was to have the students shadow a refugee for 24 hours to really get a sense of what they go through, but after weighing safety concerns, I worked with Rakeen and the volunteer coordinator at JNRC to create a "Day in the Life of a Refugee Walking Tour," which had its intended outcome. The students deeply understood, if only for a short time, what these people, many of whom are similar in age, go through.

I prepared for the day by putting on a pair of soft pants, a sweat-resistant shirt, and comfortable walking shoes. I packed a water bottle, my sunglasses, and an open-minded attitude. Before we started our walking "tour," we were introduced to Mansur, who would be our guide. As we walked to our first destination, he told us he was twenty-five and that he came to Rome from Afghanistan.

Our first stop was a center where many refugees go when they first arrive in Rome. There, they could eat one meal and apply for documents. I was surprised because it was located near one of Italy's monuments, *Monumento Nazionale a Vittorio Emanuele II*, yet the place was very discreet. It was the first door on the left of an alleyway, right behind the tram stop. There was one door to enter the building and you could not see inside through any of the windows. We asked Mansur how displaced people knew of this organization, because it seemed to be very low-key in a busy area. He told us that the main way people found out about resources were through other refugees. Everything came down to word of mouth communication. In a world where many people rely on phones for everything from navigation to a connection to their social circle, it was remarkable to ponder the challenge of arriving in a foreign country and solely relying on your communication.

Refugees do not have a GPS on their phone, if they have a
phone at all. They have to memorize directions and hope they
do not make a wrong turn in order to reach their destination.

We cut through a park and walked up a steep hill to arrive
at a place where Mansur said he sometimes ate lunch. He
said lunch was served from 11:30 a.m. to 1:30 p.m., every
day. Mansur explained that many of the places that gave out
meals only served breakfast and lunch, not dinner. Somehow
we started talking about where he wants to live in the future.
He told us, "Belgium, maybe Paris," then very quietly he
murmured "Afghanistan," and he chuckled a tiny bit.

—*Alyssa Cutcher*

A patch of dirt, a small hill, and a tree. Backdrop: The
Coliseum. Many people only see a great spot to take a picture,
but Rakeen, my guide for the day, told me that was the
last place he called home before he found the Joel Nafuma
Refugee Center.

When we first arrived at this beautiful park, Rakeen told
us about some of the "normal" things refugees in Rome have
to deal with: hiding in bushes until the park gets locked up,
looking for a warm meal, or searching for a shower within
the city center. As we walked deeper into the park, Rakeen
pointed out a marble bench. He had slept on that very bench
when he came to Rome until he had something stolen from
him in the middle of the night and he decided he could not
stay there anymore.

Rakeen took us through an area with tall grass and
wildflowers. As we walked through, he began shushing
us. There was someone sleeping in the tall grass, on top of
cardboard and under a tarp. That moment was when Rakeen's
experiences felt most real to me. When he pointed out

benches and parks, I admittedly only saw scenery. Seeing the sleeping man made it tangible.

—*Kendall Eme*

I came to a realization on Friday. Many of the refugees living in Rome have such little control over their lives. Rakeen had everything he cared about, his family, friends, and home, taken away from him in the most cruel and unjust way possible. He's been through so much in the years since he fled Afghanistan, yet he has embraced these struggles and offers endless praise for the blessings he has been given in Rome. Five hours of following Rakeen to experience a day in the life of a refugee is an experience I will never forget.

The sights and sounds of Rome are awe-inspiring, but make the city daunting to outsiders. Traffic fills busy streets as Vespa motorcycles swerve around idle cars, hosts try to fill the empty seats of their bars and pizzerias, street performers display their art, and in the midst of it all, one might also be able to pick out a refugee.

Being a stranger to Rome, taking my first steps from the Termini (train station), I would be terrified. I've already gotten lost more times than I can count, even with a map and a small amount of Italian to rely upon. The streets don't run in straight lines. Sometimes I head east, only to have the street twist and turn and suddenly I'm headed north. I'm lucky, many locals have adapted to English speaking tourists by having translations on their signs and menu. Communicating with anyone as a refugee would be incredibly difficult.

Throughout the day, Rakeen took us to the many parks and benches he has called home since he first arrived in Rome. I was taken aback when he shared the struggle and hardships he faced while he was homeless. Even though he had very few possessions, he had to constantly live in fear of being robbed. As a stranger in this city, I have an apprehension of being pickpocketed when around large crowds, but Rakeen couldn't sleep a single night without that fear. Oftentimes he would hide in parks while they were being locked, so he had at least some form of security.

Rakeen also showed us one of Rome's soup kitchens he used to regularly visit. He explained how the line would wrap all the way to the street as people hoped to get at least one meal in their stomach for the day. Rome is so famous for its food. The pizza and pasta is the best in the world. I have been struggling, knowing that my options are seemingly unlimited when it comes to my meals. I have the means to buy three meals a day, while these refugees struggle for every bite.

—Connor Simpkins

A DAY IN THE LIFE OF A
REFUGEE   BY TERYNEE BRADSHAW

Terynee Bradshaw reflects on her 'Day in the Life' experience. View video at: goo.gl/n8PMdi

Many cups of tea being prepared for the breakfast rush.

Stereotypes

A CACOPHONY OF languages permeates the crypt of St. Paul's Within the Walls, the home of the Joel Nafuma Refugee Center. Farsi, French, Italian, Arabic, English, Swahili, Housa, and many others create a Tower of Babel atmosphere. The men trickle in about 9:15 am and breakfast, a boiled egg, an apple, and a cup of sweet hot tea, is served. My students help distribute breakfast, while the clacking of the metal ball hitting the boards of the foosball table is drowned out only by intermittent shouts of joy or despair depending on who's winning. Friendly matches of Jenga, chess, and checkers are heated competitions, and the guests at the center are very skilled. Card games abound, and the buzz in the center is lively and friendly. With the exception of the languages being spoken, it would be easy to mistake this place for a college hangout on a Friday night.

At 10:15, the beeping from the newly-installed "helping next" machine invites guests to queue to receive items from the distribution center such as clothing, shoes, underwear, socks, and various toiletries. The toiletries come on a small piece of cardboard and the guests wash, shave, and lotion themselves to the extent possible in the small bathroom in the center. There are no showers. Volunteer barbers, often refugees themselves, provide haircuts for their peers.

At 10:30, English and Italian classes commence, and the classroom is often standing room only. The desire for these men to better their lives through education is apparent. They know that learning Italian will allow them to navigate the city and its bureaucracies, but learning English will allow them to complete forms, apply for jobs, and create resumes. They soak up the language like sponges. They want to know the English word for a person who is rich and does not share his or her wealth with others (greedy). They want to know the difference between "to wear" and "to dress". They want to know what separates "anxious" from "frustrated", "married" from "wedding". They are stunningly bright, often asking in Italian what a word means in English, and I feel humbled by their intellect.

In my twelve years of teaching at Michigan State University, I have never seen students so eager and motivated to learn, a desire that is not lost on the MSU students, who know how common it is for American students to skip classes and take their privileged educational opportunities for granted. The students carry notebooks of every size and shape to record their new words, often in three columns: Italian, English, and Arabic. It becomes painfully obvious how difficult English is to learn as a non-native speaker. The sounds don't make sense and the spelling isn't consistent, especially compared to the very phonetic Italian. But the learners from Ghana, the Gambia, Afghanistan, Pakistan, Cameroon, Mali, and other countries, carry on, scribbling in their ragged notebooks, which they guard like treasure, every day that English is offered.

The students learn that the guests at the center are far from the stereotypes that seek to depict them: lazy, dirty, uneducated, terrorist.

Lazy. Nasim leaves his job at the center after breakfast and goes to Centro Astalli, another refugee center operated through Jesuit Refugee Services, to volunteer working the lunch shift. After that, he works evenings at the stadium selling refreshments at sporting events, and when he's finished with his shifts there, he sells scarves or umbrellas in Rome's *piazze*, depending on the weather, often until 2 a.m. Then he is back at the center the next morning to do it all again. He is one of the most conscientious, hard-working people I have ever encountered. He never stops moving or smiling, and he never stops caring for those around him, often asking **us,** "*tutto posto?*" (everything OK?).

Dirty. Not by choice. Sleeping on the ground or on a park bench is not a clean option for anyone, regardless of skin color, age, religion, or education. Most refugees are looking for work, but the unemployment rate in Italy for those between the ages of 18 and 30 is around 40%, so refugees from a foreign country who do not speak fluent Italian often don't stand a chance. And, they have to be in the country for three years to be eligible to get a work permit, leaving many of them to appear lazy.

Uneducated. Many were successful professionals in their home countries, or studying to make a better life for themselves. Rakeen, for instance, was studying psychology before he was kidnapped and his family was killed.

Terrorist. Not long ago Rakeen had a few hours off from his new job as caretaker of an elderly man. He was hoping to spend some time outside to get some fresh air, maybe check in with friends, and run some errands. The police saw him and his backpack and detained him for over two and a half hours, questioning him to make sure he wasn't a terrorist. He has seen people move away from him on the bus and hold their belongings more tightly when he is around. The times I invited him to dine with my son and me there was a palpable judgment from servers and nearby customers in some of the restaurants and cafés we patronized, as if Rakeen didn't deserve to be there. These men hunger and thirst for the same friendship, sustenance, security, knowledge, and improved living conditions we all do, a commonality among all humans, no matter where you come from.

My task at the center this morning was to serve breakfast with Trevor and Nasim, the chef. The men would line up, hand us a meal ticket, and receive hot tea, an apple, and a hard boiled egg in return.

I thought about my own breakfast I had that morning: a banana with peanut butter and a cappuccino. Most mornings, my stomach was already growling just three hours later. I couldn't believe that an apple and a hard-boiled egg, even less than I had, was supposed to keep these men slightly full. Yet, they rolled through the line, saying good morning, appreciating and thanking us for their small breakfast.

During a lag in the line, Nasim started asking Trevor and me questions, mostly through nonverbal cues and a few English words he knew. He asked Trevor, "Do you have a wife?" which automatically made me giggle, because come on, it's Trevor. Trevor responded and in return, we asked him if he had a wife. It was extremely difficult to understand exactly what he was saying, but he started talking about his mom, dad, wife, and three children back in Afghanistan. Suddenly, he brought his hand to neck level and sliced his hand across his neck, indicating a death. I was stunned. Nasim repeated the universal sign of being "cut off" and I felt a pang in my heart.

Nasim made a gun with his two fingers and showed us multiple wounds on his lower leg. I was holding back tears at that point, but had to continue the conversation, just as he continued on in his daily life, as he casually moved on to ask me if my parents lived in America.

Nasim's whole family, the love of his life, and their three children were murdered. He lives with that every day. I thought about my own family.

Initially, I didn't understand how he continued to live every day with such positivity and hope. But, after talking to the people at the center, I realized it's either live or die. He could've collapsed and given up. But he was here, today, helping feed hundreds of other people.

You simply cannot understand the pain Nasim has felt until you look at his face as he tells the story of his tragedy. You just can't understand the pain of a refugee until you try to walk in their shoes.

—Kaila Baroff

Today was my first day volunteering at the refugee center. Mackenzie, Shelby, Megan and I walked down the stairs into the basement of the center. I immediately felt out of place. We were all smiling and refreshed from a good night's sleep. Half of the men were slouching in chairs at the tables or sitting quietly in the back room watching a projected movie on the wall. The others were huddled around what seemed to be an intense card game. I felt a sense of guilt for having been able to sleep in a bed and start my day with a warm shower.

Later, Megan and I started a game of Jenga with one of the young men. He had obviously played before because he made very strategic moves when it was his turn. We exchanged names and the countries we call home. He laughed when Megan and I practiced our Italian with him. After a couple of rounds we started to draw a crowd around the table because of our impressive Jenga skills. After the tower fell, we asked various bystanders if they wanted to join. They eagerly agreed. The two men that sat down were both from Pakistan. One young man didn't speak much English but was proficient in Italian. We exchanged basic information and he quietly spoke Italian to the others at the table. The other man was older. He was dressed well in a collared shirt and sweater vest and spoke

English well. He didn't share much about his past or his family. He was fluent in five languages, so I imagined that he was a very successful man in Pakistan. He did not mention how old he was, but he reminded me of my father. I could not help but imagine my dad in a situation like this, to reconcile a life in America with that of a refugee. It was not easy.

—Julia Attard

During breakfast, Rakeen approached me and asked if I would want to help out in the supply room for the day. I was ready to help with anything, though I did not know what to expect in the supply room. One of the volunteers, Eduardo, told us to just relax and we would figure it out.

Each JNRC member had a card that kept track of how many items and clothes they could take during a certain period, and what they have or haven't used yet. This included daily needs like razors, shaving cream, hair gel, shampoo, deodorant, cologne, baby oil, and a lot more.

It was gratifying and fun to help people in need pick out their clothes. I remember one young man saying "You choose these shoes to get girls?" as he was picking out a pair.

—Nathan DePelsMaeker

Rakeen offered us the chance to see where one of the refugees lived. It was the home of the man who served breakfast and poured the tea so perfectly it never spilled. When Rakeen asked him to show us his home, his eyes lit up. Although 40 years my senior, I struggled to keep up with him as he bustled down the Roman street and took a sharp turn into an alley. He opened the door with flourish to a shed. He was proud of his home as he gestured to the bed and showed us his few belongings. The bed was a new addition, we were told, and was propped up so you could walk through. Some of the walls were covered in poster board because not all four sides had full walls.

When it rains, the water pours in, flooding the room. Despite its flaws, he is proud of his home. Since fleeing Afghanistan, it has been the only home he has had. He asked us to take a photo while we were standing in his little home. I couldn't help but cry while trying to smile for the photo. He is proud and I am sad. It didn't seem fair that such a sweet human being was in these circumstances.

Every time it rains in Rome, at least four men will appear, trying to sell you an umbrella. Every day up until this point, I've waved them off, uninterested. What if this man had approached me on the street and I did the same to him? I would be waving off a proud, kind, hardworking man.

—*Katherine Harvey*

Rakeen in the kitchen of the center.

Listen to Rakeen tell his story by following this link: http://www.thebittersweetlife.net/podcast/episode-140-rakeen/ or read the transcribed recording. Rakeen's story may not be suitable for younger listeners.

Walking in Rakeen's Shoes

Every so often the Beehive Ho(s)tel, owned by American couple Steve Brenner and Linda Martinez, will host storytelling events and invite community members to participate on a certain topic. The following is what Rakeen shared with the audience.

THANK YOU VERY much everyone. My name is Rakeen, I am from Afghanistan, from Kabul. I was born in Kabul, I had a very comfortable life there. I was born into an educated family, my mother was a teacher, my father was an engineer. Also, I graduated from school. I studied two years of psychology. Unfortunately, I couldn't finish. In that period, I was very interested in writing, especially in school. When I was in school, when the teacher was giving us homework, to write something, some article about winter, about peace, about love, about anything. I was writing too many pages, two pages, three pages, four pages, and the teacher was getting tired and saying, please Rakeen, as short as possible. I was really interested to write and write. My father knew that I was really interested in writing, I think, and he introduced me to someone who was a writer and he encouraged me more, and my first book was published after I graduated school, and I started psychology. I was very happy. Then I started writing again and again. In fact, we had a very comfortable life.

How it happened, that my life changed. Maybe, many of you don't know about Afghanistan, what is going on. Not only the problem of Al-Qaeda and the problem of the Taliban. We also have a mafia, kidnappers in Afghanistan. They are working, looking to get to some people who are rich, who have too much money, and they are kidnapping their son, daughter, they're kidnapping and asking for money. If they don't send money, they have their ears, have their finger or something cut, send to the family, to force the family to send them money. This is an easy way for them to steal money from the rich people.

I was also a victim, I had an ice cream shop, part-time. I was going to my shop sometimes. When I was on the way to go to the ice cream shop, it was early morning, and a car came with black glass, and some people came out with masks, and they put something in my nose. Sorry about my English, I can't, I just want to tell what I mean. When I opened my eyes, I was in a very small room, my hand was closed, and some people with masks came and they gave me the phone to call, tell me to ask my parents to send us money. I knew that that much money that they were asking from my parents was difficult for my family, even for my father, he was trying to sell the car, the house, it was not possible, they were asking for about $500,000 from my father. And they knew that. They knew that if they didn't send the money, they would kill me, punish me. It happened before. One of my neighbors, six months before the day that I had been kidnapped, they kidnapped my neighbor and they were cutting his ear and sending to the family: if you don't send money, next time we will kill him. And the parents were really trying to gather the money, to send it, to save their children. Next time they cut his finger, and sent it to his family. And the family couldn't provide that much money that they wanted. And then they killed him, and put him in a bag, and put him in the back of their home. They were doing that for other people that they were kidnapping, it was a lesson for others to send money as soon as possible. This is something they were doing. This was their business. I knew that it was very dangerous for me to be here, but my father was really trying to make them busy, and my father was telling them, I'm trying to sell my house, I really put my house for sale if someone comes, I will sell my house and I will send you the money. When I was there, almost four months I was in their 'jail', and they were beating me ... too much ... and they were recording video of the beating, and still I have the signs of their beatings in my legs and in my back, and I was yelling and there was beating, and they were recording. I still have some of the recordings, I still have the photos that they had been taking and sending to my family to force them to be sorry about me, and to send money.

I don't know, it was a miracle, something happened, every time they were coming to give me food to eat, small bread, water, it was given to me so that I did not die. They were opening my hand and I was able to eat and go to the toilet. It was just one time. On that night, I knew that tomorrow, they would maybe cut my ear or cut my finger to send to my family. I knew that. I knew that it would happen because it was very late and my father was trying to make them busy. There was a small window at the top. They had opened my hand and they forgot to close it back. And they went and they closed the door and I was also kind of pretending that my hand was closed. And they didn't understand that they didn't close my hand. So it was a good opportunity for me, so I started jumping for the window. It was a small window, and I tried to first enter my one shoulder and my head. That shoulder was really difficult to get inside the window. And I kept pushing myself, you know if you were in such a, I don't know, if you know that you will die, and you try your best to rescue yourself, even if you are hurt, even if you .. you don't care, you are trying. This shoulder was very difficult, but I endured, even the bones were showing when I went through that window. Everyone can see the bones. Also, the last time, I don't know what you call here – when I got through the window, it was two floors down, I was hanging in the window, when I see, it was two floors. And I try my best and push myself and just threw myself from the window. And by God, I don't know it was really a miracle, that I just rolled and fell with my legs first, and I hit the ground, and I wake up, and I stand and start running.

I see that the street has cars crossing, I know that there is a street, and I'm just running, I just keep running. I arrive and I was totally bloody, even before, when they were hitting me, there was nothing to wash, there was nothing to wash my hair and especially in this place they were hitting me, they were beating me in the back. There was blood in my ear, and other places. I stopped one car, and it was a taxi. First he heard and said, what happened? I said please, please bring me to the nearest security or police, where it is, please. And he was a very good man, and he gave me a ride to the nearest,

A photograph of Rakeen taken by his captors.

in fact, the office for the National Directorate of Security. So they bring me there, and I enter the office, and the guard said, What happened to you? I said I am Rakeen, I have been kidnapped please help me to go and talk to the people who are inside. They let me go inside and they knew I had been kidnapped because my father reported everything to the police, to the security agency, to everywhere, that my son had been kidnapped. They ask my name, when I gave my name they knew I had been kidnapped. So they ask me please, as soon as possible, if you can go with us you will be safe, just show us please, where the house was, where it was that I had been kidnapped. I said yeah, of course, I can do that for you. They also asked the taxi driver to bring us. I was born in Kabul and I know the area in Kabul very well, so I knew where it was. So we went there, and they covered that area and I told them that other people from those kidnappers were coming in the morning. So they were waiting a little bit, but they thought that maybe they would know, so they start the operation to that house, but in fact there was resistance, there was defending, and there was fighting between this group and the police. Two people had been arrested, three were killed. Many of them were not here, they got the news that something had happened here. So I came to my home and my father, everyone, was very happy and for about one or two months we were very happy and we were thinking that it was the end of the problem.

Then we got some blackmail, some email, from that group, again. And they were warning me that if I had escaped from their 'jail,' if I had got away, why did you not go to your home? Why did you report us to police? And they came and they damaged and they killed many of us.

When I saw this my father was very scared about what we should do. So we rented out our apartment and moved to a different place in Kabul. We knew that this place was not safe for us. Maybe this group would come and do something to us. In fact, three people of them had been killed. In Afghanistan, there is revenge. Anyone who died, a brother who was killed or someone, they are trying to get revenge on someone. They are killing, unfortunately they are some people like that. Not all, but some people are like that.

So, we've been some other place. My mother had a heart attack a long time before, sometimes when the heart attack she was sick, and we were bringing her to the hospital. My father was with her one night and the next night I was with her. One night my father, the next night I was with her. We needed to take care of her so something would not happen. So one night, when I wanted to go to her, that night my little sister – I also wanted to say, I had two brothers and two sisters – they were smaller than me. My brother's name was Faisal, and my sister's names were Michelle and Mariam. And if I translate in English: Mary, mother of Jesus. She was trying to go with me to the hospital. I told her that she was seven years old, I told her that it was not necessary to go, hospital is not the place for children, the next time, tomorrow, if I can I will bring her to the ice cream shop, and we will be happy. It was the first time that she was really pushing to go with me, I don't know, kind of that maybe she knew something. So, I was in the hospital when the kidnappers found my place, and they came at two o'clock, two o'clock at night, everyone was sleeping. My father, my two brothers and two sisters, and they just shoot, and kill, everyone.

My family.

I was in the hospital, and the neighbors called, and they came to the hospital, and they first came to me and they asked me that this happened to your family, and in fact, I didn't want it, but that my mother would know about it, because she had a heart attack, so I didn't want her to know about this because it was dangerous if she knew because something bad would happen to her. I was hiding for a long time. I couldn't manage to go see their grave and to brave that kind of ceremony. I was just trying to be with my mother. I was very sad and could not control my crying when I was with her, but I was just trying

because of the health of my mother to not say anything and that …

Yeah.

So, when my mother was little bit feeling better, the doctor said you can tell her now, she's feeling a little bit better, and I told her. It was the very, very saddest moment in my life. Me and my mother was hugging each other and crying, crying. I can't imagine how can I explain how I was feeling at that time. So, another sadness was that when we were calling to all our relatives, uncles, anyone that had a relationship with us, let us bring you home for a few days, until we can find another place out of the city, we said no one was answering our phone, no one was trying to contact us, we were just at the hospital. No one. In fact, my father was helping many people, but no one came to us, bring us anything. At one point, I know that they were afraid, that they were thinking maybe the kidnappers would find their home and something would happen to their family as well.

It was one of my friends, who was at school with me, he was my classmate, he was friendly with me, like a brother. I called him and told him you are my only hope, please help me, we are in the hospital and we have no other place to go. Nowhere is safe for us. Please. And he told me Rakeen, my home, you can come any time if you want. And he came and it was nighttime when he brought me there, to his home. I was there for about six or seven months, I was in their home. Then my mother asked me how long should we be here, hiding like this? We would not have any future here. You have to go out, to foreign countries, to go make your life, then invite me, and I will come and I will be also fine with my heart attack and everything will be OK. In fact I was not trying to go away from my mother, I always trying to be with my mother, but she forced me to go and make a future because how long would I be here, useless, nothing will happen.

So, I came to Europe, I came very easily to Europe, I didn't come by car, we had money and we gave the money to someone to bring me easier to Europe. My first country when I arrived was Norway. When I arrived to Norway, unfortunately there was some problem with Afghan refugees in Norway. Norway was not accepting refugees at that time because they had some contract with Afghan government, they had signed that contract to send back all refugees to Afghanistan, because now Afghanistan is international security forces there, everyone is safe there. They were not accepting any refugees, especially Afghani refugees.

Even with my video records that I had, the photos, documents from governor, proving that my life was in danger, but there were telling me that we know that your life is in danger in Kabul, but you can go to Kandahar, to Helmand, to other cities and you can live. I was thinking that what kind of human rights is this? They're coming in my country and they're telling human rights human rights human rights, they're blaming all kinds of groups in my country, but when I'm here, they know that my life is in danger in Kabul, they will kill me and kill my mother, so they are telling me that you can go live in Kandahar or Mazar, or some other place. They give me negative answer so I give them liar, I am trying to find documents to make me safe somewhere, that my mother will be safe. So after four years I was there, I saw that it was useless to be here, and my mother was sick. They wanted to deport me with the second negative answer, I knew that they would send me back to Afghanistan, so Italy was my only option. In fact, if I explain about Italy, I have two points, one positive and one negative. Positive points about Italy is that, for me, it's really helped. Really helped. If Norway would deport me back to Afghanistan I don't know what would happen with me and my life. But Italy was the only country that was not sending back people. If you have fingerprints in one European country, so you cannot apply to another European country. So if you apply to a second European country, they will send you back to the first country. So Italy was the only country that was not sending back refugees to the first. And I came here, many problems and difficulties that I faced here I can't imagine, so three months that I came here I was living in a tent in the park, my first experience of my life that I was sleeping in a park, for three months.

I had a comfortable life in my house and I can't imagine, just thinking about human rights, when I was hearing about Europe, about human rights, about equality, about goodness, about these things. After three months I spoke to police and they looked for a camp for me, and I find a place to be in a camp. When I was in a camp, I was sleeping with 10 people in a small room. I don't know if you can imagine sleeping with 10 people in a very small room. Someone is snoring, someone is coughing, someone is talking. I didn't have good sleep. And there was no good food. And the water was cold if you wanted to take a shower, the water was totally cold even during the winter, this is not humane. This is not humanity. We do not deserve to live like that. If you are giving documents to someone to live like that that is not good. And also I find that JNRC center in that moment when I was there. When I find this center, I meet Monica, she is sitting here, she is a psychologist, she is very talented and a very good woman. And on that time, my mother also had heart attack, and she died. After six months that I was here, my mother also died. I was very totally, kind of dead, dead, like dead person. I was not like alive, I did not have any feelings, I was just crying, in every park I was sitting like crazy, I was talking to the trees, I wanted to talk to God, why would this happen in my life, why would you take everything in my life from me? My mother was my only hope, why did you take her? Like a crazy. But when I come to this center, and I met some wonderful people, and they gave me some hope, and I'm really happy for them. After, when Monica had some meetings with me, she introduced me to the artisan groups

I have family. I am a person, I can be someone, I am a human being, I am very thankful from the deep of my heart now I have brothers, sisters. I am in a family now. I am not like the person that I was before. And the last point that I want to focus on is about anti-immigrants, and anti-Muslims. Those guys who are anti-immigrants or anti-refugees, 85% percent of them are anti-Muslim. I, as a Muslim, we should not follow some other groups doing in the name of Islam, or Muslims. The main point is about the knowledge. They don't have knowledge about my religion, just they hate and just they see what is going on. I never find any verse, any verse in the Quran to say to kill a Christian, to go to heaven. This is all programmed, this is all games, all political games. As a Muslim I want to tell you: We love Jesus, peace be upon him. Muslims and Christians have so much together. We must not let our disagreement overshadow the fact that we have so much together. For example, Muslims and Christians believe in Jesus, peace be upon him, no Muslim is a Muslim without believing in Jesus, peace be upon him, we believe that Jesus was one of the mightiest messengers of God. We believe that he gave life to the dead, and we believe that he performed many miraculous deeds, and we believe that God raised him up into the heavens, and we believe that Jesus will return a second time back. We have common beliefs with our Christian friends. Remember that Muslims and Christians make up more than half of the world's population. If we combine our efforts in good, we can serve ourselves and human kind all the better. Thank you very much for joining us tonight.

**Mackenzie Van Vleck playing chess with Rakeen.
He is currently undefeated at the center.**

Matthew Wigglesworth ("Wigs") and
Zane Wilson working breakfast.

Learning Through Experience

A KEY COMPONENT to the Sales Leadership Minor at MSU is the focus on experiential learning. If we are to train the next generation of professional salespeople and future business leaders, they must learn to communicate effectively with other people. All kinds of people. They have to be able to have a conversation, to develop rapport, to establish trust, and to relate to others on a human level. They must learn how to interpret body language and communication styles and to overcome barriers to effective communication. They have to be able to ask the right questions to get at the heart of a client's situation to offer productive, efficient solutions. They need to be able to think critically and navigate conversation with people who are vastly different than they are, who come to the table with different backgrounds, cultures, and perspectives. They need to become creative problem solvers. Often it is easier to teach these skills when the students' attention is captive and they are removed from their East Lansing bubble.

One of the many skills required of an effective salesperson is empathy. To be a creative problem solver, the students need to be able to put themselves in the shoes of whomever they are working with. To achieve proficiency, we practice with sales role plays, simulate sales management situations, and utilize questioning techniques to marry what we learn in the classroom with what the students experience in the "real world". In Rome, in addition to creating marketing plans, social media strategies for business, and learning about the importance of corporate social responsibility, we walk a day in another person's shoes and we fast.

For students who have never experienced true want, the murder of family members, being adrift at sea for days or weeks at a time, or food insecurity, fasting is one way to develop empathy. I ask the students to fast for a day to the extent they are able without jeopardizing any underlying health issues. This year the fasting coincided with Ramadan, a month in the Muslim religion where participants go without food and drink from dawn until sunset to commemorate the first revelation of the Quran to Muhammad.

Food insecurity is common among refugees. Many don't know where and when they will get their next meal.

Today, I tried fasting.

I felt absolutely terrible. I have a morning routine—I normally eat a banana with peanut butter and some coffee. This morning, I skipped my routine and I felt out of tune both from deviating from habit as well as from hunger. I spent the morning at the refugee center and went on a grocery-shopping excursion to the market with Rakeen. As we walked through the stations, I just thought about what I wanted to eat at that moment. Mostly, I yearned for a cheeseburger. As the morning progressed, I was absolutely exhausted.

I know something about myself: my whole demeanor changes when I'm hungry. It's very noticeable. I get crabby, light-headed, impatient, and just plain out of it.

But being hungry every day is reality for so many of these refugees. They lack proper nutrition, they lack food altogether. Yet, in the refugee center this morning, I only experienced friendliness and compassion from these men. You wouldn't be able to tell if they had gone without food.

—*Kaila Baroff*

I started fasting first thing in the morning because I wanted to see how I would be affected by having to go through my whole day without the security of having food. I always start my day with a cup of coffee, so it hit me hard.

Within an hour of waking up, I had already begun yawning and had developed a slight caffeine-deprived headache. The hunger came later, and I began to feel very sluggish. It made it hard to pay attention and I kept thinking about wanting to take a nap in order to try and replenish some of my energy.

What I noticed most was how often everyone talks about food. When you're well-fed, you don't notice the conversations about good restaurants as much. Today though, I was frustrated in spite of myself, listening to classmates describe the meals they wanted to get that day. I knew I wouldn't be able to join them, and it even made me a little bit angry to listen to them talk. It was no fault of their own, and they continued with their conversations, unaware that I was fasting.

It made me realize what it would be like to starve in a world filled with billboards advertising fast food, pictures of food outside restaurants and everyone talking about their meals. It's even worse in a "foodie" culture like Italy.

As I became more lethargic, my thoughts became very bitter. I couldn't focus and I began to overthink everything. I was focusing on a lot of interpersonal relationships and I was getting frustrated with everyone talking. It had made me pretty grumpy and I was ready to be alone.

I thought about the men I had met at the refugee center, and whether they felt lethargic during the day. I was having a lot of trouble focusing, and I didn't even have any pressing short-term needs, because I knew for a fact I'd be able to eat once the day was done. Trying to figure out how to get a job, find a place to stay, or learning a new language in this state would be practically impossible.

We often talk about how brave refugees are. This exercise is a reminder that they are brave in more ways than one. Taking on the world is hard enough with a full stomach and clear mind.

—*Katherine Harvey*

My roommate and I fasted for 24 hours today. It's safe to say that our entire day revolved around the lack of food. It started off easy. I missed my morning cappuccino a bit, but still felt completely fine and functional. As the day went on, I continued to grow more and more irritable. All of my thoughts and energy were focused on food. I noticed I had become more quiet and reserved. My normal social habits diminished. I noticed the people I was with made little effort to reach out to me in my cranky and exhausted state of mind. This experience gave me a great amount of understanding into the mind of a refugee. This was only one day for me, one assignment. For them, it's not a choice. They are stuck with this hunger and exhaustion every single day. I know how hard it made easy every day activities for myself; I cannot even fathom living every day with that exhaustion.

—*Mackenzie Van Vleck*

Today I fasted for 11 and a half hours … and it changed my life.

I prepared for this experience by stuffing my face with pasta late at night the night before. A full stomach is a happy stomach, right? I was pretty confident I could pull this off with ease. I woke up at 8:00 a.m., showered and headed to the refugee center.

Ramadan had begun. This helped me not think about food as much. When we left the center though, all bets were off. My friends immediately grabbed a piece of pizza and the struggle began for real.

The next seven hours had me preoccupied with one thing, and one thing only: food. I tried to focus on other activities to get my mind off food, even considered a nap and a workout. It helped for a bit, but after I woke up, I regretted my decisions. I was exhausted and my body was drained.

In the hot Italian sun, it felt like every step was another step closer to passing out. I have fasted before, but never to this extent. It solidified my perception of the refugees I had been working with, how strong they are, both mentally and physically.

I look around at the world in a different way now. I couldn't shake the thought that I've overused the word 'starving' so often. It almost feels like a curse word now.

—*Kyle Gomes*

Kendall Eme reflects on fasting and her experience in Rome. View video at: goo.gl/t2L0qf

Sempre in Giro

According to the UNHCR, there are currently 65 million people searching for refuge worldwide. It would take 867 consecutive days, or 2.37 years, to fill Spartan Stadium on Michigan State University's campus, which seats around 75,000 people, to reach 65 million.

Rakeen lost his family in a brutal, heinous way, a way in which most of us can never begin to comprehend. He was kidnapped off the street as he walked to work, was ripped away from his family and home, and was held for ransom for four months. He was starved and beaten while his captors photographed and videotaped him screaming and writhing in agony. The only thing worse than the beatings he endured was the fear of when they would begin cutting off his body parts to send to his family to expedite delivery of the ransom. It reads like a plot from a horror film, or more aptly, a terror film, one in which he was the terrorized protagonist.

Then, in retaliation for reporting them to the authorities, members of the kidnappers' gang shot and killed his father, two little brothers, and two little sisters in the middle of the night as they slept. He never saw them alive again, he never saw their bodies after their murder, and he wasn't able to attend their funerals as they were laid to rest. Before leaving the hospital with his mother, Rakeen reached out to family and friends to take them in until they could make other arrangements. However, fear of retribution was stronger than compassion, and everyone they knew turned them away. His last hope was a school friend who lived outside of Kabul, and finally they found refuge.

Frightened by the turn of events, Rakeen's mother begged him to get out of Afghanistan because she could not bear to lose him too. He did not want to leave her behind, but he knew he was in danger the longer he remained. He vowed to send for her when he could, but before he left Afghanistan, Rakeen and his mother visited the gravesites of their murdered family members. It was the closest they would ever come to reaching closure.

The price tag for the human trafficker to get him out of Afghanistan to Europe, a place known for humanitarian values, was $24,000. The flight, his first ever, stopped in Frankfurt, Germany, then to Sweden where a pre-arranged car waited to drive him to Oslo, Norway, where he lived for four years. While in Norway he talked with his mother as often as possible and tried to get permanent asylum. In the meantime, the Afghan government signed an agreement with Norway to send all refugees back to Afghanistan, for it was now deemed "safe." Supported by video footage and photographs of his torture, Rakeen appealed several times to the Norwegian government to allow him to stay but they denied his pleas, saying he could settle somewhere in Afghanistan in a place other than in Kabul. He was scheduled to be deported.

Rakeen felt his only choice was to go to Italy, where refugees seeking asylum are not refused if they can demonstrate that their lives are in danger if they were to return. He fled to Rome. During his first three months there, Rakeen slept in a large tent in a park for Afghan refugees, but after being robbed a couple of times, he took to sleeping on

To read a New York Times account of Rakeen's time in Norway, follow this link: goo.gl/8zIgIK park benches or in fields near the Coliseum. Sleep often did not come and peace of mind was a luxury he longed for. He appealed to the police for assistance and was directed to a camp for refugees that had thirty-nine rooms, ten men to a room. The camp accepted guests from the hours of 7:00 p.m until the following morning at 9:00 a.m, at which point every day they had to leave. Sleep deprivation continued from the snoring, coughing, talking on cell phones, and the crawling and biting of the bed bugs that plagued the rooms. Rakeen's only respite from the nocturnal insects came from shining the light from his cell phone on them, so he could squash them between his fingers. He still bears a skin irritation on his neck from their bites, three years later. The desperation of his circumstances quickly turned to despair.

Food in the camp was tasteless, usually bland pasta with a little sauce, or rice, but in the face of extreme hunger he ate what was offered, longing for the flavorful dishes loaded with spices he dreamed of from home. Hot water did not exist in the camp, and he was chronically ill from taking cold showers. Funds set aside by the government for refugee services were discovered to have been diverted to members of the *Mafia Capitale* (Capital Mafia), crooked politicians who partnered with the mafia to award bogus contracts in order to line their own pockets. A wire tap of one politician's phone conversation recorded him saying that he could make more money preying on refugees than he could trafficking drugs. The business of exploiting the weak and marginalized was (and is) thriving, casting refugees aside as collateral damage and a source of revenue generated from continuous war and conflict.

Some days Rakeen was able to have a hot shower, but obtaining it meant an hour-long trip outside the city to a mosque. Back at the camp, he would stand in line for hours to access one of the two washing machines that serviced the other 389 residents if he wanted clean clothes. Each load of laundry took up to an hour to wash, and the queue was endless. Other days began by taking a bus to get in line at a soup kitchen for lunch, then killing time walking or sitting in a park until it was time for dinner. It was routine for Rakeen to be stopped, prompted for his documents, questioned, and frisked by police who suspected him of dealing drugs or other criminal activity. Days ended by returning to the insect-infested bed he called home after the camp re-opened in the evening. Every day was dismal and exhausting just to get the basic necessities for survival. There was no end in sight and he felt as if he would be *sempre in giro*.

I am currently wrapping up the fourth week of the second best decision that I have ever made, the first being going to Michigan State University. I have changed. My perspective has changed. My attitudes have changed. This program has changed me in ways I didn't think imaginable. We're not done yet (thank the good Lord) and I plan on making the most of it. In my fourth week of volunteering I got the privilege of going grocery shopping with Rakeen. This was my first real opportunity to bond with him. One of my favorite things about Rakeen is that he is a hugger. No matter if it is the first time he is meeting you or the last, he gives you a warm embrace and lets you know that he cares about you and loves you. Being a hugger myself, I appreciate someone who understands the value of a good hug and enjoys every lasting second of it. My journey with Rakeen on Wednesday started with a hug and ended with a hug. Nothing monumental happened on our routine trip to the market, but some of the realizations that I made were of the monumental sort.

Talking to him about what he has endured made it more real for what this is all about and why we are here. It was little comments like how he can only listen to peaceful music because music that might come off as a little aggressive can remind him of what he has gone through. My appreciation for that beautiful man has increased tenfold since first arriving in Rome. I was moved when he finished his performance at the

Talent show last night. His standing ovation was one reserved for purple heart winners, and let's face it, he basically deserves one.

You really don't know someone until you walk a mile in their shoes is a saying with tremendous truth and power. During the first week of this program we took that literally by following in the footsteps of refugees as they persist in their quest for survival. This week we starved ourselves and fasted to understand what kind of resources and practicalities the refugees were working with on a day to day basis. It is truly amazing how the refugees can persevere through each and every day with so few resources at their disposal. I fasted for 24 hours from Monday night to Tuesday night and it was excruciating. The hunger absolutely ate away at me throughout the day. Concentration decreased exponentially the longer I went without food. I felt my vision fade slightly and energy deteriorate. I was a shell of my former self, and that's just after one day. I can not even imagine the struggles that refugees go through every day with no nourishment and the never-ending uphill battle that is their struggle for survival.

I have a whole new perception about refugees and who they are. They are people who need to be loved and helped, not feared. Refugees are people who need to be embraced because sometimes they are like Rakeen and give the best embraces of all.

—*Trevor Ploucha*

Lost and Found

RAKEEN WAS LOST. He experienced post-traumatic stress, despair, exhaustion, sleep deprivation, and depression. Who wouldn't, given the same set of circumstances? The losses came in every imaginable sense: home, freedom, a comfortable life, family, education, his small business, dignity, peace of mind, personal safety, and in the end, the inevitable loss of his love, Marine.

Rakeen and Marine met in the 10th or 11th grade, he recalls. He ran into her as she was coming out of the market with many things to carry and she bumped into him, dropped her bags, and then asked him for help. He walked her home, carried the bags, and he asked for her number. They began seeing each other, but their dating was very different than what is considered normal in western countries. He never touched her for the four years they were together. Touching a woman who is not your mother, wife, or fiancée isn't done in his culture. He recalls that she was a "nice girl, a polite girl, she had a good character," and he loved her very much. They were looking forward to a long life together. The photographs of Marine are stunning: long, flowing, wavy brown hair; smoldering, kind, dark brown eyes; and a beautiful, full smile. They were to marry after college and begin their lives together. Rakeen's mother contacted Marine's mother about the match, as is customary, but after his kidnapping and the retaliation against his family, Marine's family withdrew their consent because they feared she, too, would become a target for the kidnappers. Rakeen, again, was devastated. He had lost everything he thought was possible to lose. Then six months after his arrival in Rome, he received the call from his friend in Afghanistan who was caring for his mother, telling him that she had died of a heart attack. They laid her to rest with his father, sisters, and brothers. There was nothing left to lose. He had been a refugee for four and a half years, and the depths of his despair could go no deeper.

> What would you take with you? View video at: goo.gl/et345i

After learning of his mother's death, Rakeen recalls that grief and hopelessness overtook him. He was "totally out of control, even I decided to (commit) suicide. Two nights I could not sleep but the third night when I go to sleep I saw my mom in a dream. She comes closer to me and hugs me and said this to me: 'don't give up.' After that dream I feel (ready) to live and try again to continue … I need to fight with problems and difficulties and memories with (a) smile and keep myself sure that I (don't) belong to the past anymore. This was the message from my mother while I was very worried. She told me 'don't give up.'"

Rakeen began to take advantage of psychological counseling available at JNRC, and credits Monica, the psychologist who works with guests at the center, with helping him through some of his worst despair. Often ignored in the news reports and sound bytes *vis-à-vis* refugees is the emotional toll being a refugee takes. Numbers are reported, terrorist images are perpetuated, fear is fueled, but few seem to give the briefest attention to the emotional and psychological toll the pandemic of forced displacement takes on its 65 million victims. Dr. Richard Mollica, professor and psychiatrist at Harvard, has spent the bulk of his career working with traumatized refugee populations from Cambodia, Rwanda, South Africa, and Chile, among others, and has written an insightful book for both lay people and professionals called *Healing Invisible Wounds: Paths to Hope and Recovery in a Violent World*, a book my students and I read and discuss prior to arriving in Italy. Dr. Mollica also runs the Harvard Program in Refugee Trauma, a hybrid certificate program that entails two weeks in Orvieto, Italy, and an additional five months of instruction on line for practitioners working with refugee populations.

> Did you know that trauma may be carried genetically?
> Read more: goo.gl/YDsKF9

JNRC has psychological services, music therapy, and art therapy groups to assist guests with processing what they have endured, but the groups are mostly facilitated by volunteers, and the need often can outstrip the resources. The guests produce beautiful artwork, which is often displayed around the center and many pieces have been turned into greeting cards to be sold with their artisan crafts. Special exhibits and markets are held to increase awareness and to sell a variety of items, including peace flags, jewelry, baskets, and ornaments. Most recently, the artisans have begun making clothing from beautiful fabrics from their home countries. Selling their artisan crafts is one small way in which they can learn a new skill, feel productive, earn a bit of money, and donate a portion of the proceeds back to the center to ensure the sustainability of its programs.

In spite of the devastating losses Rakeen has endured, compelling him to thoughts of suicide, he found support at JNRC through his network of mentors, artisans, friends, his new-found family. Concurrently he found a sense of purpose and a way to contribute to his community. He found a way to push through when he wanted to give up. He found that which had been lost, that which was most precious to him. He found himself.

Watch a JNRC video featuring Rakeen: goo.gl/6KAh7S

The author and her son, Stephen, departing for an excursion.

Mackenzie Van Vleck talks about her Made in Italy experience. View video at: goo.gl/g7ZUfE

Reflections

OFTENTIMES STUDENTS FLY through a semester of classes without taking the opportunity to reflect on what they have seen or observed with those who experienced it with them. They simply move on to the next thing. Experiential programs allow information to become part of the students' DNA, part of their "muscle memory," like being in a living laboratory. It allows them to become one with the "what" and the "why" of what they are learning. The theoretical comes alive, hypotheses are tested, and student perceptions are transformed because they observe familiar paradigms through a different lens. A lens that is foreign. One that seems out of focus. One that challenges what they know about themselves and the world they thought they understood.

Thus, reflecting on our experience was exhilarating and rewarding, yet overwhelmingly bittersweet. In past years, we would hold our farewell dinner at an Italian restaurant, but this group had grown exponentially and learned unreservedly with each other and the guests at the center, and we wanted them to be part of our farewell. Rakeen suggested an Afghani feast and asked that our last day together not be a sad affair but, instead, a celebration we would always remember. And it was. The food Rakeen and Nasim prepared was out of this world, the students shared their reflections with Rakeen personally, and Piero, the manager of JNRC, was asked to DJ a dance party for us. The poignant culmination of our time together resulted in laughter, sharing, tears, joy, and sadness that overwhelmed us all, but we parted with an unshakable *esprit de corps*.

On our last day at the JNRC, we were all able to share our thoughts and feelings of our experience volunteering there. We wrote short (but sweet!) notes, and then read them out loud. Some shared moments of laughter, others were more sentimental and personal. As I sat around a long table accompanied by great friends, new and old, I heard many things that resonated with me. I connected most with the unexpected changes we had all experienced. When we arrived here, we expected to impact someone's life, to positively impact the refugee center. Instead, *we* were changed. The knowledge, perspective, and love we had gained from being at the refugee center was far greater than we imagined it would be.

This experience has solidified my passion for service. To see the world from a different perspective was eye opening. It made me think differently about a lot of things, especially the refugee crisis that is occurring around us every day. It is so easy to hear about, and yet completely ignore when it is not happening at your front door. Being able to get to know Rakeen allowed me to a put a face and name to the term 'refugee.'

One of my greatest takeaways is to never take anything for granted. There are so many things that go unappreciated in an average day. A new pair of socks, toiletries, or even a place to sleep at night. I have been very fortunate to never have to worry about any of these things, and this was a good reminder of how much I take for granted on a daily basis.

—*Megan Casler*

I cannot believe that I am already sitting at my desk at home typing my final reflection. I knew that six weeks wasn't a long period of time, but I never expected that it would go by so quickly. I also never expected to develop the relationships

I have developed or retain the knowledge I have learned in such a short time. The 17 strangers that sat with me in pre-departure meetings are now considered my family and the experiences I have had taught me more about myself and the world around me than four years in college has.

Friday was our last day at the Joel Nafuma Refugee Center. Walking into the center for the last time was tough. I could feel the tears welling up at the back of my eyes. It is so hard to say goodbye to the people that have taken my world and flipped it upside down in the best way possible. Without them I would be stuck in my peaceful, quiet, naïve little bubble and that is not where I want to live my life. It is so simple to promise that you will come back to visit and will keep in touch, but it is also so simple to get lost in your daily life. There are so many times that I make a point to reach out to an old friend or visit a family member but I always let something else take priority. I never do it on purpose or in spite of the person, but I tend to push it off until next week or next time and sadly there isn't always a next time. However, I want to prioritize the relationships I have built at the JNRC and keep in contact with the people I have met and learned so much from.

Over the past six weeks we have learned about the circumstances of many refugees that come to the center each day. We have learned about the tragedies that the refugees have overcome and in some way we have helped them grow and encouraged them to keep moving forward.

I have learned the impact that an open mind and a listening ear can have on a person that is going through a difficult time. Being acknowledged and accepted is not something that these refugees experience on a daily basis. They are often looked down upon and treated disrespectfully, as if they don't belong. We were able to welcome them into a safe place where they were treated as humans, not numbers. I have always known that love is powerful but experiencing it firsthand at the JNRC from both the volunteers and refugees has been overwhelming. The love and compassion that was exchanged between everyone makes me believe that there is still goodness in this crazy world. The refugees have gone through some of the most horrendous experiences and come out of them with love in their hearts. I have learned that no matter how hard or unfair life is, hate is not the answer. That is what I want others to know. I wish I could bottle up my experiences and my emotions and give them to my friends and family so they can begin to understand the negative impact of a closed mind.

Rakeen had each of us write a brief reflection of our time spent at the center that would be shared at our last dinner together. It was so incredibly difficult to summarize and effectively express all that I have learned and felt in the past six weeks. I wanted Rakeen to understand what a huge impact he had made on our lives and how much we care about him and the relationship we have built. When the time came to share our reflections, I made the mistake of sitting next to Rakeen. I listened as each of my peers reflected upon their experiences and watched as Rakeen absorbed every last word. It was difficult to watch him listen and react to the beautiful things that were being said, knowing that we would be over 4,500 miles apart in less than 24 hours. Rakeen fully opened his heart to us and I am sure it was 18 times as heartbreaking for him to watch us leave as it was for us to leave him. Instead of exchanging goodbyes we exchanged "see you laters," hoping that it was true.

My hope for the future is that I am able to transfer the knowledge I have gained in Rome and at JNRC into my daily life and to be able to practice kindness, love, and acceptance. I hope that by practicing these things those around me do the same. I want to spread awareness of the refugee crisis and teach people why it is important to understand what is happening in the world even if it doesn't affect them directly. I know it is not going to be easy and I know that people will challenge my thoughts and beliefs, but I am dedicated to giving refugees the love and respect they deserve.

—*Julia Attard*

My two life mottos are "What's meant to be will always find its way" and "Teamwork makes the dream work." In the past few days I've been reflecting a lot on how my mottos have applied to our last six weeks in Rome. First, I think that there is always a reason for why you meet certain people. Either you need them to change your life or you end up changing theirs. After spending time with refugees at the center, and getting to know you, Rakeen, my heart has been touched. Before I came to Rome, I was uneducated about the global refugee crisis. I would see the headlines, but it did not directly affect me so I did not pay attention to the problem. After individualizing refugees and meeting so many fearless men like Rakeen, who were forced to flee their home due to struggles that are sometimes incomprehensible, it has caused me to become passionate about something I never would have expected to influence me before this program. I've never met a strong person with an easy past, and I can confidently say that Rakeen is the strongest person I have ever met in my entire life. You have been through hell and back, and somehow you still wake up everyday with a positive attitude. When I return home I'll miss you tapping on my shoulder and then hiding. I'll miss hearing you say your favorite English slang terms like "Gotcha," or "Can you hook a brother up?" but most of all I'll miss seeing your big smile every time someone makes you laugh. Thank you for feeling comfortable to share your story with us, and thank you for whole-heartedly loving every one of us as your brothers and sisters.

My second life motto about teamwork is directed towards all of you other beautiful people. Over the past six weeks we have done something special; we've created. We've created marketing plans, a shoe drive, video blogs, a talent show, "that's amore" and welcome-to-the-stage rhymes, but most importantly, we've created memories. We've created big moments and we've created little moments. It's taken a lot of group collaboration to accomplish everything we've done, and we've all stepped up to the plate with an open and confident mindset. Thanks for making dreams become reality; this study abroad program was better than anything I ever could have imagined thanks to each and every one of you.

—Alyssa Cutcher

As I begin to wrap up my time in Rome and at JNRC, I have begun doing a lot of reflection on how my perceptions and attitudes have been changed by my experiences here. I have seen the most change in my perception of refugees and my impact on them as a volunteer. It's taken time but I feel like I now fully appreciate the work we have been doing. It's honestly been one of the most rewarding experiences of my life and I hope that my efforts make a lasting impression on those I've volunteered with.

When I was first introduced to the volunteering aspect of the program, I wasn't sure what to make of it. I had seen the news stories covering the refugee crisis and heard of the hardships that many faced while fleeing their country. I understood the reasoning behind our actions; these are some of the most cast aside people in society, facing extreme oppression. What I didn't understand was how my role as a volunteer for six weeks would make any difference. I've learned a ton but the biggest lesson that will travel home with me is that no matter how small one's contribution is, it always has an impact, often larger than you could imagine. Some refer to this phenomenon as the butterfly effect: the flap of a butterfly's wings could set off a chain reaction that results in a major alteration in the world. I am beginning to see this phenomenon with my own eyes as refugees come and go throughout the center. It's small contributions I have helped make, like serve breakfast, host a talent show, tutor English and mathematics, and simply being a friend that has a lasting impact. When I leave Rome I will continue to act and become a figure in my community to evoke change.

It's difficult to communicate and express everything I have learned. I've learned so much about history, culture, and of course, myself. I wanted to make a conscious effort to return to America a different man. At that time, I wasn't sure what kind of man I would become; all I knew was that I didn't want to spend six weeks living in another country just to return home with the same mentality. I have seen myself grow to become a more outgoing person. I now crave to learn about the details that have shaped others' lives. This has been especially rewarding at JNRC, as I have met the most amazing people with some of the most frightening stories. Every day I spent interacting with these people I was surprised by the courage they exhibited, trusting that their lives could improve. They aren't looking for handouts. They are intelligent, motivated individuals that have been kicked to the bottom of society and are clawing their way back up. From Rakeen, I learned a valuable lesson that things that I take for granted, like my education, family and home, are what motivate them to look toward the future with optimism.

—*Connor Simpkins*

> To see a couple of the acts from the talent show the students organized with students from St. Stephen's International School to benefit the guests at JNRC, follow this link: goo.gl/RrP7i6

It is hard to describe what being able to volunteer at the refugee center meant to me. I feel like I have explained it in so many different ways. I've tried to articulate it in writing, in video blogs and to my friends and family. However, overall I think how I showed what it meant to me was how I act today. Before coming to Rome I knew nothing of the refugee crisis. I would see numbers on the screen but then they would disappear and I would go along with my day. I knew people in the world were not as fortunate as I am. After travelling to Zambia, Africa four years ago I got a taste of that. However, it began to get blurred in my world today. I focused on finding a job and spending time with my friends and before I knew it, where I was going on a Friday night was increasingly important to me.

Now my eyes are more open to the world around me. I am not scared by the man carrying all his belongings on the subway. Instead, I think of him and what may have happened to get him to where he is in that moment. Overall I think I learned that everyone in this world wants relationships and we all have things in common. I enjoyed going to the refugee center because I knew I was going not to go to see the "refugees" but I was going to see my friends.

Rakeen has taught me more than he could have ever realized. He truly appreciates the little things in life. He taught me that every day is different and that you have to make a conscious effort to make every day a good day. Watching him get upset over us leaving was really hard for me to see. How can you convey that you care about someone so deeply and that he is not just a friend but that he is family now? Families have to be apart sometimes but that doesn't make them any less of family. He is our family now. I also learned so much about the goals of the men in the center. They all had unforeseen situations in their life like we all do and they get up every morning because they refuse to be shaken by it. Having the opportunity to spend time with them was a pleasure and a privilege.

My three biggest takeaways from this experience are that no matter where you are from or what you have experienced in your life, everyone wants love and friendship. Second, no matter what cards you are dealt, it is up to you to go into every day with a positive attitude, and finally, that refugees are not numbers or clumps of people; they are individuals who are a products of their situation, often in the wrong place at the wrong time.

—*Katherine Harvey*

I'm sad to see this program come to an end. I can't believe six weeks went by that quickly. Saying goodbye was so much more difficult that I ever could've imagined. Our final night at the Joel Nafuma Refugee Center is one that I will remember and cherish forever. Enjoying the wonderful food that Rakeen prepared for us, laughing with all of my friends, and listening to the takeaway words that everyone wrote for Rakeen was beyond powerful. Dancing with everyone in the program and at the center, singing as loud as we could, crying together, hugging and saying our goodbyes was priceless.

I wish I could keep in touch with everyone I've met, but I know that's unrealistic. I do know that I'll be in touch with Rakeen. I've already chatted with him over Facebook.

It's hard to describe the impact this experience had on me. As the new Community Service Chair on the Executive Board for our club to raise refugee awareness, I plan on becoming more involved with volunteering while getting others involved. Listening to the stories refugees tell, seeing their pain, their pride, their strength, and their determination, and feeling for them as they interact with us, will stay with me for the rest of my life. This entire program was much more intense than I had ever expected, but I honestly wouldn't trade it for the world.

I am ashamed to admit that I didn't used to pay much attention to what was going on in the world. Needless to say, I've already changed significantly, and not just due to how much more world news I'll be consuming. Not only was this program educating and eye-opening, it was humbling. Having the family that I do, living the life that I live, in the area that I do, I am truly blessed and I would like to show my gratitude more than ever

—*Mackenzie Kreitz*

My first lesson with Sean taught me more than a year's worth of classes combined. It taught me the importance of seeing your surroundings instead of just looking at them. It taught me the value of reflecting upon the way that things make you feel in a particular moment and sharing that with others. It taught me to pause to find the symbols and deeper meaning in everything. I learned that I no longer believe in coincidence. My classmates and I began a ritual in which we would stand in a circle and take deep breaths when we were in unfathomable places. We did this so that we could try to comprehend our surroundings instead of rush through them. We wanted to understand and appreciate things on a deeper level, and I am so grateful that we learned how to experience the past few weeks instead of just seeing things at surface level. Sean taught me the importance of finding the "why" in everything.

From Jennifer, I learned that you can never love too many people. I learned that family is not always blood. I learned that even though we cannot change the world, it is important to try to make a difference. If you can make someone happy for a day, or even a couple of minutes, it is worth the effort. I will no longer be able to turn a blind eye to the things happening around me and I will speak up for things that I believe in. Jennifer challenged me to jump off the cliff of my comfort zone and realize that there is so much more to the world. Thanks to her, I will never look at the world the same and I will never stop pushing myself to experience more of it.

—Shelby Roland

I couldn't be happier that I dug deep instead of just skiing through this incredible experience. It's easy to come oversees and play tourist on a surface level. I feel so fortunate that I've been a part of a program that encouraged me to do otherwise. There is no possible way I will walk away from this experience and be able to view the world in the same way. After being here and feeling so independent, I am nervous to face the "real world" back home.

I am returning home a different person. I have new eyes to see the world. I have a new passion to expand on: improving the lives of refugees. I have an incredible new family who will continue to encourage me and grow with me. And I have this program to thank for that.

—*Mackenzie VanVleck*

I am a firm believer that the best goodbyes are the hardest because that means you experienced something worth having. The goodbyes I have experienced on this trip have been some of the hardest and toughest ones I have experienced in my life.

Saying goodbye to the people I met at the refugee center was heartbreaking because I knew that we were on such different paths in life and I very well might never see them again, even though they taught me so much about love and perseverance. I will never forget the look on General Nasim's face as I saluted him one final time, or as I gave my last wave to Rakeen and he gave one back before breaking down and sobbing.

On our final night in Rome I went around and one by one told everybody on this program how much I loved them and how much they mean to me, as well as what they have shown and taught me while abroad. Dry sleeves were at a premium.

I exit this program with a newfound sense of confidence and self-assuredness. I know for a fact that there is nothing that I cannot handle and that there is nothing that I should fear. I will never let fear dictate what I do. I have a better understanding of how innately good people can be and how misconceptions are the greatest enemy of the human race.

Made in Italy changed my life. It has shaped me into the person I want to become. I know I am not where I need to be yet with my life, but this program was a huge catalyst into getting me there. I am more confident. I am more understanding. And I am more loving. I owe all the future success I will have in my lifetime to the six weeks I spent in Rome with the greatest group of people that I have met.

—*Trevor Ploucha*

The Journey Doesn't End Here

OUR EXPERIENCE HAS ended, but the global refugee crisis hasn't. In fact, it has been exacerbated by policies put into place by governments, ours and others', as well as the firestorm of negativity, misunderstanding and rhetoric that has enveloped our society. Retreating into ourselves and embracing a "we versus they" mentality only serves to fan the fire of fear and misunderstanding.

Education is key. Education breeds understanding. Education allows us to see for ourselves.

I challenged the students to get involved, to educate themselves, and to share their knowledge with others. Michigan is third in the top ten states in the U.S. that relocate refugees seeking asylum in the United States. The vetting process to come into the U.S. is extremely thorough and often takes two to three years of investigation before allowing an individual to come into the country. Asylum seekers are screened and re-screened, checked and re-checked. When they arrive in Lansing, Michigan, a hub for refugee resettlement in Michigan State University's back yard, they are met at the airport with an interpreter who speaks their native language. They are taken to a home that has been prepared especially for them by volunteers with donated furniture, housewares and linens, and they receive assistance finding jobs and situating their children in school. They are assigned mentor individuals or families who help them acclimate to the area and navigate tasks of daily living that are foreign to them. Employees like Judi Harris, John Karasinki, and the staff at St. Vincent Catholic Charities' Refugee Resettlement work tirelessly to assist these people. The Lansing Refugee Development Center offers a multitude of services, including English language instruction for adults and after school tutoring for refugee children new to the area. They also run an independent soccer league to allow children to acclimate and find support among their peers, a far cry from the "welcome" refugees encounter in other parts of the world.

Follow this link to see an infographic by the UNHCR that explains refugee resettlement in the United States: goo.gl/KeeqKW

Now that my students are familiar with the global refugee crisis, it is impossible to revert to blissful ignorance. They realize that information about refugees depicted in the media and among political spin doctors is often based on generalizations and stereotypes rather than first person interaction and fact. The students understand that they have a moral imperative to share what they know with others, indeed, the purpose for this book.

In class we created the marketing, sales, social media, and communication strategies to get Rakeen's story to a larger audience, in the form of this book. The students knew I started a non-profit organization for the benefit of political refugees last spring called "Welcome the Strangers," and they used their own transformation from ignorance to advocacy to start a student organization at MSU called "Spartans Welcome the Strangers." I am honored and humbled that I get to call this experience part of my job, and I am thrilled to have the opportunity to expose another group of students to JNRC this summer.

Our appeal to you, Dear Reader, is not simply to trust our word for it, but instead to spend a day in another person's shoes and invite them to share their story with you. Rakeen's story is only one of 65 million. Get involved with or contribute to local, national, and international organizations that support refugees. In the back of the book there is a list of resources, websites, and books that shed light on this issue. It is our hope that you will educate yourselves and take action: volunteer to teach English to people who are anxious to learn, help coach a soccer team for children who may have a difficult time assimilating to a new culture, take the time to look into someone's eyes and listen to them relate the circumstances that brought them to your country. Ask them what is important to them. Ask them about their families. Ask them about their dreams. Ask them what they miss from home.

What you may find is that their answers transcend the rhetoric, stereotypes, biases, and fear through which we have been conditioned and deconstruct barriers that separate us to give way to our common humanity. You may find that what motivates us as human beings, explained most famously by Maslow's hierarchy of needs (physiological, security, love/belonging, esteem, self-actualization), is universal and transcends religion, politics, language, and skin color. You might just find that by pushing the limits of your personal comfort zone that you open yourself to global understanding, and you may learn more about yourself than you thought possible while you walk a day in someone else's shoes. And then we hope you celebrate what you have learned and share it with others.

Dear Rakeen,

Hi, i'm Eveline and i'm twelve years old. I was th
when you were telling your story at the American
school of Barcelona with your other friends. (Mayb
you remember me, in the last presentation, for 7th
and 8th graders. I was the girl with curly hair. I
gave you a big high five at the end.) Well I just
wanted to tell you that you are so brave! Your
story could be a really good movie (I nearly cried!)
You are so brave for many, many reasons and here
are some of them. You didn't see your family for 4
months, you escaped, you told the police, you help
your mum, you traveled for months, you sleep in
a park... but most importantly you didn't give up.
When you left to escape, they didn't let you in, so
instead of giving up, you went further to Italy. You
really made me think about what truly is important
and you really inspired me. Thank you for sharing
your sad story with the world. I hope from the
bottom of my heart that you will live a happy life
with your new family. Don't forget that you are
a real HERO ♥♥♥ Don't give up!

Lots of love, Eveline. ♥

Letters to Rakeen

MOST AMERICANS DO not have first hand knowledge of the global refugee crisis, so to combat that Jill Drzewiecki, former volunteer coordinator at JNRC, began fundraising in the summer of 2015 for a small group of refugees in Rome to do an educational tour in the United States to tell their stories. Michigan State University was to be one of their stops. However, securing tourist visas for political refugees was a long shot, and the American Embassy ultimately rejected the applications. They reasoned that a refugee coming to the United States without a work contract or a bank account in Italy would have no reason to return to Italy. But money had been raised for travel and accommodations, so undeterred, the group instead went on a European educational tour six months later. One of their stops was the American School in Barcelona, Spain.

Rakeen told a middle school classroom full of students what he had endured at the hands of kidnappers trying to extort money from his family and the retaliation he faced as a result of exposing them. Shortly thereafter he was shocked to receive an envelope in the mail at JNRC with his name on it, an envelope filled with loving, supportive letters from children who were affected deeply by his story. A selection of those letters is included here. Jill, by the way, is now a Campaign Development Coordinator for Mercy in Motion, a fundraising campaign at Jesuit Refugee Service International, located in Rome. The tagline for the campaign is "Providing Education, Investing in Peace" with the end goal to educate refugees in camps around the world so that the intellectual potential of human beings facing displacement does not go untapped. View the video at: goo.gl/kPclwb.

Dear Rakeem,

My name is Noa. I just turned 13 years old, and I come from Israel. I wanted to write you a quick letter to say that I am really thankful to have had the opportunity to sit down and listen to your story. Your journey from leaving your home all the way to Rome, was so inspiring, and had a

huge impact on me. You made me realise, how tough it is to be safe. It is so tough leaving your country behind, and it is so tough to sail on boats and walk with no food and water, and it is really tough to live in refugee camps. I realized how so many people in the world are suffering from this problem, and I had no idea about it. This experience really opened my eyes into the world, and I started to notice what is going on around the earth. Additionally, I want to tell you that what you did was really brave of you. You took risks to escape Afghanistan, which is something that I am too scared to do. You inspire me so much and you are a big role model. I also wanted to add that I can relate to you a bit. I know how it's like to live in a country where there is war. Since I come from Israel, I have experienced stuff like this quite a few times, and it's scary. Hearing bombs, and police cars is really terrifying, but for you to be able to handle that and be so brave about it, is so mindblowing. It is so hard to believe that you were so young and experienced such horrific things in your life. To conclude, I wanted to tell you that ASB will always be part of your home, and you are welcome here anytime. You are a huge inspiration and we loved hearing your story, as it made us realize what really is important in the world. Thank you so much,

Noa

Dear Rakeen,

My name is Marina and I am 12 years old. I am really thankful for having the opportunity of being able to listen to your story. I am really sorry for everything, but I am really happy to hear that you have a family now. It was really fascinating for me to see that you never gave up, and you always perservered. It was really touching to hear your story with details on podcast. I was also really inspired by how you went through so much, but you ended up in a better and safer place. You are an amazing role model to me, showii that you should never stop trying and you will find success. Your hard work has payed off and now you are happy.

P.S.
If you have an e-mail adress, mine is:
███████████████████████████

Kind regards,
Marina ████████

Dear Rakeen,

Do you remember me? It's your bro, Luis from the American School of Barcelona. First I want to start with, I heard your story. Every word you said melted my heart, you're my idol. You are the strongest person I have ever met, even stronger than Hulk. You want to know why I think this? Because what you did takes a lot of strength and courage, because if they would of caught you, luckily they didn't, i'm sure that it wouldn't of ended well. To add on, I know that everything was extremely hard for you. But you had a goal, to escape your country, and go to another one where you would be welcomed and taken care of, and in the first place it didn't work out. What made me realize the most was that after being in Norway and not being able to stay you didn't give up, you kept fighting to achieve your goal, and never gave up. Finally you did it. This makes me realize, that if I ever have a goal, and it doesn't go out as planned, then I should keep trying just like you did, until I achieve it. I would love to see you again anytime, I can go to Rome. But what would be awesome is for you to please come back to Barcelona, and spend family time with me, and mom, sister, and brother. My mom, and family and I really mean it you can come home, and we can go do a lot of fun things, bigger brother and little brother stuff, because remember, you are my bro forever.

You are amazing!

Sincerely,

your bro,

Luis

Feb 5th 2016

Dear Rakeen,

I thank you so much with all my heart for coming to visit our school in Barcelona. It was truly an honour to hear your story during your presentation. Sometimes people don't realise how lucky they are, but thank you for opening our eyes to the reality of life. At the end of your presentation I took part in a group hug and I think that was the first time that I felt like a human. Humanity has really changed and I think that the feeling of being bare and participating in something so special really motivates me. Your story inspires me to help others as much as I can. I am very curious about how you are living in Rome. You are an amazing person and I respect you so much. What you have gone through is remarkable and I hope that other people will notice as well. I hope that one day humans will begin to think about others and not just themselves.

Where do you live?
Did you enjoy Barcelona?
Please send love to Maiga, Saho and Adama.

Sincerely,
Isabella ███████

2-5-16

Dear Rakeen,

You have been through so much, and yet you are still able to conquer your past and be happy, despite everything you have been through. Your courage is unmatched and I will forever see you as a role model.

Thank you for coming to our school and being able to share your story with us, despite how hard it must have been. You are an incredible man and I am in awe of you and your accomplishments.

While I listened to what you said, I almost thought that it couldn't be true, like it was something out of a movie. However, when I realized that you had really suffered through this, I realized how fortunate I am to be living in the safety that I have.

After your and the other refugees' visit, never again will I take for granted any of the luxuries that I had never realized were luxuries. Thank you for coming and sharing your story with us.

From an admiring student,

Baz ▮▮▮▮▮

Tyler Kramer and 4 others commented on this.

 Rakeen ▮▮ with Katherine Harriet and 13 others.
23 hrs ·

It was One of the best moments of my life in 2016 to met these super awesome people. I'm so lucky to have you as friends in my life. Wish you all the best in 2017.
Love and miss you 🤍🤍🤍

👍 Like   💬 Comment   ➤ Share

👍❤️ You, Poppy Pizzichelli, Shelby Roland and 39 others

View 1 more comment

 Kaila Baroff Love you Rakeen! Happiest 2017 to you 😊
Unlike · Reply · 👍9 · 23 hrs

 Trevor Ploucha Rakeen you are an inspiration to us all and not a days goes by where you don't come across our minds. All the love.
Unlike · Reply · 👍9 · 21 hrs

 Kyle Gomes We are all honored to have you as a friend Rakeen, I think we can all agree being in Rome with you was one of the best moments of our lives as well. Have an amazing 2017 brother
Unlike · Reply · 👍6 · 17 hrs

 Tyler Kramer We miss you dearly, Rakeen and the time we spent with you will be cherished for years to come. Wishing you a healthy & happy 2017, and everyone else we had met in Rome with you!
Unlike · Reply · 👍4 · 16 hrs

 Love you all! What a life-changing experience we had together!
Love you Rakeen!

About the Co-Authors

Julia Attard graduated from MSU in December of 2016 with a B.A. in Communication and a minor in Sales Leadership. She accepted a full-time position with C.H. Robinson as an account manager. Julia was a member of Global Sales Leadership Society and is a founding member of Spartans Welcome the Strangers.

LinkedIn: http://linkedin.com/in/julia-attard-15a010b4

Kaila Baroff is pursuing a degree in Communication with a minor in Sales Leadership. She has a passion for traveling and experiencing new cultures. She loves being with her family and friends, and she is forever proud to be a Spartan. Kaila is a founding member of Spartans Welcome the Strangers and serves as Vice President for the group. She has accepted an internship this summer with Altria.

LinkedIn: www.linkedin.com/in/kaila-baroff-66a797113

Terynee Bradshaw is a proud senior at Michigan State University studying Communication and Sales Leadership. She is a founding member of Spartans Welcome the Strangers, Global Sales Leadership Society, The Spartan Success Program, The Advantage program, and F.A.M.I.L.Y. (Forget About Me, I Love You). Tery enjoys mentoring, volunteering, teaching, and creating lasting relationships inside and outside of these organizations. Tery refers to her time in Rome as by far her best experience at Michigan State, and spending time with Rakeen and all the refugees at JNRC has forever changed her life.

LinkedIn: https://www.linkedin.com/in/terynee-bradshaw-7064a785

Megan Casler is pursuing an Advertising degree with a minor in Sales Leadership. She is on the Executive Board for Alternative Spartan Break, and she is a member of Global Sales Leadership Society and is a founding member of Spartans Welcome the Strangers. Meg is heavily involved in intramural sports at MSU and plays on soccer, volleyball, softball, and basketball teams. She has accepted a full time position with Align Technologies after graduation in May 2017.

LinkedIn: https://www.linkedin.com/in/megancasler

Alyssa Cutcher is a junior at Michigan State University majoring in Communication, and she is pursuing the Sales Leadership Minor. Her interests include playing tennis and volleyball, watching MSU and Detroit sports teams, and listening to country music. She is a founding member and Secretary of Spartans Welcome the Strangers, and supports changes for the betterment of refugees struggling around the world.

LinkedIn:
https://www.linkedin.com/in/alyssa-cutcher-207622133/

Nathan DePelsMaeker has a major in Kinesiology and minors in Sales Leadership and Health Promotion. He enjoys experiencing life with the people he loves. Nathan is very involved in his fraternity and other activities around campus. He is an active member of Global Sales Leadership Society and Spartans Welcome the Strangers. GO GREEN!

LinkedIn: https://www.linkedin.com/in/
nathan-depelsmaeker-103a0611b

Kendall Eme is majoring in Communication with a minor in Sales Leadership. She loves watching the Chicago Cubs and Blackhawks, playing tennis, being a student leader, and playing with her Cavalier King Charles Spaniel, Conan. She has accepted an internship at PepsiCo in Indianapolis for the summer of 2017. Kendall is a Residence Hall Assistant, a member of Global Sales Leadership Society, and is a founding member of Spartans Welcomes the Strangers.

LinkedIn: https://www.linkedin.com/in/kendall-eme-a5bb95107

Kyle Gomes has a major in Kinesiology and a minor in Sales Leadership. His interests are in sports, spending time with friends and family, and traveling and expanding his knowledge of the world. Kyle is a founding member and President of Spartans Welcome the Strangers.

LinkedIn: https://www.linkedin.com/in/kyle-gomes-118724114/

Katherine Harvey graduated in December 2016 with a degree in Communication and a minor in Sales Leadership. While at MSU, she interned with Jennifer Rumler, was involved with Global Sales Leadership Society, and was a founding member of Spartans Welcome the Strangers. Her interests include traveling, eating great food and spending time with her friends. She has accepted a full time position with BASF in their sales professional development program.

LinkedIn: https://www.linkedin.com/in/katherineharveymsu

Tyler Kramer is from West Bloomfield, Michigan, and is working toward a degree in Communication with a minor in Sales Leadership. He plans to graduate in May 2017. Tyler is interested in pursuing a career in the healthcare industry with a focus in pharmaceutical or medical device sales. He is honored to have contributed to *Walking in Rakeen's Shoes* and is responsible for Spartans Welcome the Strangers' social media marketing. In his spare time Tyler loves to stay active, discover new music, travel, and visit alpaca farms with his family.

LinkedIn: https://www.linkedin.com/in/tyler-kramer-a0899584/

Mackenzie Kreitz is a Communication major with a minors in Health Promotion and Sales Leadership. Mackenzie is passionate about family, religion, close relationships, and philanthropy, and she is the Community Service Chair for Spartans Welcome the Strangers. She strongly believes that everything happens for a reason.

LinkedIn: https://www.linkedin.com/in/mackenzie-kreitz-589243100

Anna Mazzara is a junior Advertising major with a minor in Sales Leadership. She enjoys traveling, learning about new cultures, and meeting people from all over the world. She has a secret passion for photography, karaoke in her car, and petting as many dogs as she can. Aside from schoolwork, Anna is interested in social media development and brand promotion. After participating on the Made in Italy study abroad program Anna was instrumental in co-founding Spartans Welcome the Strangers to raise awareness at MSU of the global refugee crisis.

LinkedIn: https://www.linkedin.com/in/anna-mazzara

Trevor Ploucha is a Mechanical Engineering major with a concentration in Biomechanical Engineering and a Sales Leadership Minor. He loves Spartan sports, fine dining, reading, and elite levels of working out. Trevor is positive, energetic, and emotional, and he is someone who strives to bring out the best in everybody he meets and never backs away from a challenge. Loving life is always the first step. Living it to the fullest is always the next. Trevor has accepted a full time position after graduation May 2017 as a process engineer with Danaher Corporation in Orange, CA. He is a founding member of Spartans Welcome the Strangers.

LinkedIn: https://www.linkedin.com/in/trevor-ploucha-06b522ab/

Shelby Roland will graduate in May 2017 with a Bachelor of Arts degree in Communication and a minor in Public Relations. Shelby is a Co-Founder and VP of Marketing for Spartans Welcome the Strangers and handles press releases, manages social media accounts, and promotes events. Her other interests include running, reading, anything involving Harry Potter, listening to boy bands and working with those who have special needs.

LinkedIn: https://www.linkedin.com/in/shelby-roland 860106b3

Connor Simpkins is a senior majoring in Finance with a minor in Sales Leadership. Connor has accepted a full time offer from Edward Jones Investments and will be participating in their Financial Advisor Career Development Program beginning in the summer of 2017 in St. Louis, Missouri. Connor is a founding member and Treasurer of Spartans Welcome the Strangers.

Mackenzie VanVleck is studying Advertising with a minor in Public Relations. She is the fundraising chair for Michigan State's Spartans Welcome the Strangers. When she's not working on her studies, she enjoys making music and volunteering for Leader Dogs for the Blind. She looks forward to continuing work for SWTS during her senior year at Michigan State.

LinkedIn: www.linkedin.com/in/mackenzie-van-vleck-aa2b38127

Matthew Wigglesworth, during the creation of this book, was completing his senior year at Michigan State University, studying communication, sales and entrepreneurship. Although not on the executive board of the Spartans Welcome the Strangers, Matthew was one of its founding members and was part of the inaugural meeting that sparked the idea for the group. Outside of school and SWTS, his interests include start-up entrepreneurship and digital marketing, among other business related topics.

LinkedIn: https://www.linkedin.com/in/matthew-wigglesworthba5726126

Zane Wilson is an Advertising senior with the Sales Leadership Minor. He loves to travel and spend time with family and friends. Zane is a proud Spartan and loves to share his experiences with new people. He is a member of Global Sales Leadership Society and is a founding member and Marketing Chair for Spartans Welcomes the Strangers.

LinkedIn: www.linkedin.com/in/zane-wilson-a358501

Afterword

While Rakeen's life today does not resemble what it did seven years ago when he fled Afghanistan, the challenges are far from over. His family is still gone and dreams continue to jolt him from a sound sleep, leaving him with the profound sense of loss, like a clip from a film that plays and replays the tragedy over and over and over on a continuous loop.

Rakeen has worked odd jobs here and there, painting, cutting grass, working as an artisan, and last fall he was able to land a job as a live-in caregiver for an elderly man, which provides a roof over his head, food on the table, and money in his pocket. However, Rakeen is a highly social person, who now lives in relative isolation with the man he cares for. He does not complain because he has it better than most, but there is a distinct sadness in his voice. He does not have a contract, and he is two years into his five-year humanitarian asylum. He wonders when he will no longer be a refugee. He wonders when he might start a family of his own. He wonders when he will finally be able to get on with his life.

And when the elderly man is no longer living? Where will Rakeen go and how will he earn a living? Will he be back at square one? What happens when his five years of asylum expire? Rakeen's life has been in constant upheaval for seven years. His circumstances have improved dramatically, yet he still walks in the shoes of a refugee, *sempre in giro*.

Resources

They Poured Fire on Us From the Sky by Alephonsion Deng, Benson Deng and Benjamin Ajak

goo.gl/1nmAIs

Healing Invisible Wounds: Paths to Hope and Recovery in A Violent World by Richard F. Mollica

goo.gl/aiCbzr

St. Vincent Catholic Charities, Lansing, Michigan:

http://stvcc.org/

http://stvcc.org/services/refugee-services/

https://www.facebook.com/St.VincentCatholicCharities

Joel Nafuma Refugee Center, Rome, Italy:

http://jnrc.it/

https://www.facebook.com/JoelNafumaRefugeeCenter

Centro Astalli, Rome, Italy:

http://centroastalli.it/

https://www.facebook.com/CentroAstalli/

Jesuit Refugee Services, Rome, Italy:

https://en.jrs.net/index

http://jrsusa.org/

https://www.facebook.com/JesuitRefugeeService

Caritas Internationalis:

http://www.caritas.org/

https://www.facebook.com/IAmCaritas

UNHRC:

http://www.unhcr.org/

https://www.facebook.com/UNHCR

Lansing Refugee Development Center, Lansing, MI:

http://www.refugeedevelopmentcenter.org/

https://www.facebook.com/RefugeeDevelopmentCenter

Welcome the Strangers:

https://welcomethestrangers.org/

https://www.facebook.com/welcomethestrangers/

CPSIA information can be obtained
at www.ICGtesting.com
Printed in the USA
FSOW03n0456010417
32442FS